Russian Political War

T0383676

This book cuts through the misunderstandings about Russia's geo-political challenge to the West, presenting this not as 'hybrid war' but 'political war.'

Russia seeks to antagonise: its diplomats castigate Western 'Russophobia' and cultivate populist sentiment abroad, while its media sells Russia as a peaceable neighbour and a bastion of traditional social values. Its spies snoop, and even kill, and its hackers and trolls mount a 24/7 onslaught on Western systems and discourses. This is generally characterised as 'hybrid war,' but this is a misunderstanding of Russian strategy. Drawing extensively not just on their writings but also decades of interactions with Russian military, security and government officials, this study demonstrates that the Kremlin has updated traditional forms of non-military 'political war' for the modern world. Aware that the West, if united, is vastly richer and stronger, Putin is seeking to divide, and distract, in the hope it will either accept his claim to Russia's great-power status – or at least be unable to prevent him. In the process, Russia may be foreshadowing how the very nature of war is changing: political war may be the future.

This book will be of much interest to students of strategic studies, war studies, Russian politics and security studies.

Mark Galeotti is a senior non-resident fellow at the Institute of International Relations Prague, and a Jean Monnet Fellow at the European University Institute in Florence, Italy.

Russian Political War
Moving Beyond the Hybrid

Mark Galeotti

Routledge
Taylor & Francis Group

LONDON AND NEW YORK

First published 2019
by Routledge
2 Park Square, Milton Park, Abingdon, Oxon OX14 4RN

and by Routledge
605 Third Avenue, New York, NY 10017

First issued in paperback 2020

Routledge is an imprint of the Taylor & Francis Group, an informa business

Copyright © 2019 Mark Galeotti

The right of Mark Galeotti to be identified as author of this work
has been asserted by him in accordance with sections 77 and 78 of the
Copyright, Designs and Patents Act 1988.

British Library Cataloguing-in-Publication Data
A catalogue record for this book is available from the British Library

Library of Congress Cataloging-in-Publication Data
Names: Galeotti, Mark, author.
Title: Russian political war : moving beyond the hybrid / Mark Galeotti.
Description: First edition. | London ; New York, NY : Routledge/Taylor &
Francis Group, 2019. | Includes bibliographical references and index.
Identifiers: LCCN 2018055159 (print) | LCCN 2018056701 (ebook) |
ISBN 9780429812101 (Web PDF) | ISBN 9780429812095 (ePub) |
ISBN 9780429812088 (Mobi) | ISBN 9781138335950 (hardback) |
ISBN 9780429443442 (e-book)
Subjects: LCSH: Hybrid warfare–Russia (Federation) |
Russia (Federation)–Military policy.
Classification: LCC UA770 (ebook) | LCC UA770 .G25 2019 (print) |
DDC 355/.033547–dc23
LC record available at https://lccn.loc.gov/2018055159

ISBN 13: 978-0-367-73175-5 (pbk)
ISBN 13: 978-1-138-33595-0 (hbk)

Typeset in Times New Roman
by Newgen Publishing UK

Contents

Acknowledgements

This book derives from a report prepared in 2016, which led to the publication of an earlier and shorter version as *Hybrid War or Gibridnaya Voina? Getting Russia's Non-linear Military Challenge Right* (Mayak, 2016). I am grateful to the foundation that supported the original research for being willing to see it developed into a new form, and for Routledge for taking it on. In addition, I must express my appreciation to the European Council on Foreign Relations (ECFR) for allowing me to draw on a report I wrote for them in 2017, *Controlling Chaos: How Russia Manages Its Political War in Europe*.

Since the original draft of *Hybrid War or Gibridnaya Voina?*, my thinking has developed, the available sources expanded and I had the chance for follow-up conversations in Moscow and beyond, including invaluable encounters with Russian and Western officers and officials eager to tell me what they think I got wrong and right the first time round. My thanks to all of them, and to many more. All such projects involve not so much standing on the shoulders of giants as raiding their libraries and eavesdropping on their conversations. For direct assistance and indirectly for especially helpful conversations, I am indebted to Natalia Antonova, Jānis Bērziņš, Keir Giles, Toomas Ilves, Michael Kofman, Edward Lucas, Johan Norberg, András Rácz, Ekaterina Shulmann, Ben Tallis, Brian Whitmore, Katherine Wilkins and no doubt many others, including those interlocutors in Moscow who understandably preferred not to be named. Anna Arutunyan and Simran Maker were especially generous with their time, reading through a draft of this book and making invaluable suggestions.

I must thank New York University for supporting the original research project, the Institute of International Relations Prague at which it was developed, the anonymous reviewers who provided much useful commentary and the Robert Schuman Centre at the European University Institute, in whose elegant confines I completed this project, as a Jean Monnet Fellow. I would like to end with a shout out to War on the Rocks (http://warontherocks.com/), an essential source for some of the best and most lively (and sometimes iconoclastic) discussion about emerging military issues.

Terms and abbreviations

AP   *Administratsiya prezidenta*, Presidential Administration
FAPSI   *Federal'noe agenstvo pravitelstvennoi svyazi i
          informatsii*, Federal Agency for Government
          Communications and Information
FSB   *Federal'naya sluzhba bezopasnosti*, Federal Security
          Service
FSO   *Federal'naya sluzhba okhrany*, Federal Protection
          Service
GRU   *Glavnoe razvedyvatel'noe upravlenie*, Main Intelligence
          Directorate
GU   *Glavnoe upravlenie*, Main Directorate (official title of
          GRU since 2010)
KGB   *Komitet gosudarstvennoi bezopasnosti*, Committee for
          State Security
KSSO   *Komandovaniye sil spetsial'nykh operatsiy*, Special
          Operations Forces Command
MVD   *Ministerstvo vnutrennykh del*, Interior Ministry
SB   *Sovet bezopasnosti*, Security Council (also sometimes
          Sovbez)
Spetsnaz Special forces (*Spetsnial'nogo naznacheniya*, of special
          purpose or designation)
SVR   *Sluzhba vneshnei razvedki*, Foreign Intelligence Service
VDV   *Vozdushno-desantnye voiska*, Air-Assault Troops
          (paratroopers)

Introduction

The West is at war. It is not a war of the old sort, fought with the thunder of guns and the trumpet's martial sound, but a new kind, fought with the rustle of money, the shrill mantras of propagandists and the stealthy whispers of spies.

Having originally emerged as a term to discuss how actors such as Lebanon's Hezbollah and Iran's Revolutionary Guard could fight a massively superior enemy, the term 'hybrid war' has, since Russia's annexation of Crimea and intervention into south-eastern Ukraine in 2014, become, depending on whom you believe, a global threat or the moral panic of the age. Once written off as a decaying post-imperial nation, Russia is now being characterised as the West's most serious challenger and a threat to the international order. The reason for this is not so much a reassessment of its military as an alarm that Russia has developed a 'new way of war' that uses covert, deniable and cyber means to tilt the balance of power in its favour.

Moscow is certainly conducting an aggressive geopolitical campaign to assert its claims to great-power status and also undermine Western capacities to constrain it. However, the term hybrid war has now seemingly come to mean everything – from armed invasion by 'little green men' to spreading scurrilous gossip online – and, as such, arguably means nothing. Furthermore, most Western perspectives fail to appreciate how the Russians themselves understand and indeed fear what they now call, aping us, *gibridnaya voina*. Moscow considers itself rather a *target* of Western hybrid aggression. Moreover, there are different perspectives within its military and civilian national security communities. A failure to define and understand Russia's perspectives leads to academic confusion, wasted efforts and a fundamentally misinformed policy debate in the West.

The aim of this short and opinionated book is therefore not to be the last word on these complex and emerging security issues. Instead, it seeks at least to cut away some of the mythology about Russian hybrid war, using both Western and Russian sources to explore the actual nature of the challenge, how Russia at once fears and seeks to use non-military forms of coercion, and the extent to which this is simply a reflection of the changing ways of modern conflict. It draws on not just written sources but also years of conversations with Russian and Western officials and soldiers that especially highlight the way Western perspectives almost always conflate two distinct forms of conflict as understood by the Russians. While the West talks about 'a' Russian hybrid-war approach (putting aside the vexed question of whether it should be called hybrid war at all), there are actually two strands to Moscow's thinking about 'non-linear,' non-military conflict.

The Russian military subscribes to the kind of model we saw in Crimea and the Donbas, with non-military means used to prepare the battlefield before the injection of soldiers. As the Russians have been quick to spot, aspects of modern technologies and modern societies mean that a shooting war is especially likely to be preceded by a phase of political destabilisation and disruption. Yet despite overblown and alarmist claims about some special Russian way of war, even the wholly mythological 'Gerasimov Doctrine' (and I will address my own foolish part in creating this chimera in Chapter 2), in essence this is nothing new.

While many within NATO are concerned about outright Russian invasion, we ought not to be mesmerised by this chimera. The Kremlin does not for a minute plan or want the campaign it is waging against the West to turn into such a shooting war. Its aim is rather to divide, demoralise and distract the West enough that it cannot resist as Russia asserts its claims to being a 'great power.' Again, though, this is hardly something dramatically new. Bluff, subversion, corruption and threat have always been the statesman's tools of choice. Indeed, even though it is not one the Russians use, the best term for this, political war, actually has its roots in the writings of the quintessential US scholar-diplomat, George Kennan, in 1948, and he himself was drawing again on a rich historical tradition. Russia's national security and political establishment have embraced this approach, whereby non-kinetic means – information operations, subversion and the like – are a replacement for force, not its harbinger. In effect, political war is hybrid war without the eventual shooting – or maybe hybrid war is political war plus the eventual shooting.

So, is there nothing new in Russia's current array of geopolitical gambits? Not quite: the extent to which the Kremlin is relying on political war is unusual, and the world is very different. At a time when peer-to-peer military action has become ruinously expensive in political and economic terms alike, and yet in a world in which everyone is interconnected – as much through the internet and cultural contagion as money flows, supply chains and markets – political war may increasingly be the dominant idiom for state-to-state contestation. Besides, technological, social, economic and political developments all mean that, even if guns and missiles are getting more lethal, accurate and long-ranged, memes and dirty money are also ever more powerful instruments. This may not be a 'new way of war' so much as how war is fought in a new world.

What has emerged, if not novel, is at least a distinctive approach, one that combines traditional Russian strategies with the particular challenges or conditions with which Moscow must now contend. These range from the mismatch between assets and ambitions to the deinstitutionalisation of Putin's state. The book opens (Part I) with an exploration of how the notion of hybrid war took root in Western thinking and contrasts that with Russian thinking and practice. Part II then looks at Russian notions of warfighting – which are much more conventionally military than some seem to believe – and then how political war emerged, is conceived and organised. Part III then looks at the particular assets the Russians can deploy in their pursuit of operations short of all-out warfare, from the special forces and thuggish gangster auxiliaries who seized Crimea in 2014 to spies, propagandists and spinmasters. The point of trying to understand this threat is to respond to it, though, and the final part presents a series of observations and recommendations for Western analysis and policy alike. The policy aim must be deterrence if possible, but such is the nature of this diffuse and undeclared form of war that this will often be by denial – developing 'hybrid defences' – and the right mix of assets ready for a conflict that could as easily be fought in cyberspace, the courts or the financial markets as on the battlefield.

Nor is this simply a threat that will disappear as and when Putin's regime implodes or subsides, however inevitable this undoubtedly is. There are other revisionist powers in the world likely to emerge. The sooner the West adapts to the Russian challenge, the better it will also be positioned to face the one coming next after that. In that discussion, this book makes no claims to be a definitive answer, or anything like the last word, but the hope is that it can advance the debate as to what may be awaiting, just over the horizon.

Part I

Birth of a notion

1   The creation of a threat

NATO's greatest challenge coming out of the [2014] Wales Summit is
to take on two different forms of strategic challenge from the East and
South simultaneously. These challenges are composed of very different
actors, and various forms of modern hybrid warfare.

(Then Supreme Allied Commander Europe
General Philip Breedlove, 2015)[1]

A spectre is haunting Europe, the spectre of hybrid war. In the introduction to the 2015 edition of the International Institute for Strategic
Studies' authoritative *Military Balance*, for example, Russia's hybrid
warfare is described as including

> the use of military and non-military tools in an integrated cam-
> paign designed to achieve surprise, seize the initiative and gain
> psychological as well as physical advantages utilising diplomatic
> means; sophisticated and rapid information, electronic and cyber
> operations; covert and occasionally overt military and intelligence
> action; and economic pressure.[2]

This is a good summary, although in many ways what is actually being
described is a corollary of the Clausewitzian doctrine that war is politics by other means. This is that politics can also be considered war by
other means, that it is not about making deals and brokering consensus,
but imposing one's interests on others. There is already active and
sometimes ferocious debate as to whether Russia's current approach is
something truly new or not, and whether it is limited to certain specific theatres and contexts, rather than any wider evolution of military
art.[3] This very uncertainty has led to some epic examples of buzzword
bingo, such as the Baseline Assessment definition of the Multinational

Capability Development Campaign Countering Hybrid Warfare, which, with no apparent irony, says that 'to clear up conceptual confusion regarding hybrid warfare' it considers it 'the synchronized use of multiple instruments of power tailored to specific vulnerabilities across the full spectrum of societal functions to achieve synergistic effects.'[4] In other words, doing several things at once, in a way that is intended to work, to achieve a result – hardly a ground-breaking approach.

In light of such conceptual car-crashes, it is fair to ask how far this may be a threat of the West's own imagining. It is striking how US and NATO military perspectives on Russia have changed since 2014. From being all but written off as a decaying post-imperial nation of, at best, limited regional military significance, it is now being characterised as the West's most serious threat, even – in something of a rhetorical over-statement – a plausible 'existential threat.' Thus, in July 2015, newly-nominated chairman of the Joint Chiefs of Staff General Joseph Dunford placed Russia at the top of his list of military threats to the USA,[5] a view echoed by a string of other senior US military commanders.

The reason for this is not so much a sudden reassessment of Russia's military, although the neat and professional way it occupied Crimea in 2014 was a useful wake-up call, just as the deployment to Syria in 2015 demonstrated unexpected power projection capabilities. Rather, it is rooted in alarm that what has widely been called Russia's 'new way of war' bypasses or neutralises much of the West's undoubted capacities and superiorities. NATO, after all, has more combat troops and reserves than Russia, spends ten times as much on defence in absolute terms,[6] and can deploy much more advanced forces on the ground, at sea and in the air. But just as having an advantage in horse cavalry mattered little in the age of machine guns and barbed wire, so too the fear is that, as one US Marine Corps officer suggested to me, 'we spent billions preparing to fight the wrong war.'[7]

The war that soldier felt he was unprepared to fight was a hybrid one, a term that has, rightly or (probably) wrongly, become the term of art for a style of warfare that combines the political, economic, social and kinetic. (It would be tempting to offer an alternative, but as will become clear, my inclination is to believe that much of what is being called hybrid war should really simply be called 'war.') This kind of conflict recognises no boundaries between civilian and combatant, covert and overt, war and peace. Achieving victory – however that may be defined – permits and demands whatever means will be successful: the ethics of total war applied even to the smallest skirmish. Although the antecedents of such an approach lie elsewhere, current concerns very much focus on a revanchist and adventurist Russia. As Putin becomes increasingly assertive and also apparently genuinely gripped by a belief that the United States and the West are bent on undermining Russia, this has eclipsed such concerns as the turbulence in the Middle East and North Africa and nuclear proliferation as the primary concerns of NATO and its member states. However, in the process of seeking to understand and define this challenge, the West has, in a way, created it. Words have meaning, they invoke our fears and give them form and substance.

Although the term 'hybrid' had been bandied about before, it really was the brainchild of Frank Hoffman, who saw in the asymmetric clashes in Lebanon between Israel and the Hezbollah in 2006 a distinctive mode of conflict involving '[a] range of different forms of warfare, including conventional capabilities, irregular tactics and formations, terrorist acts including indiscriminate violence and coercion, and criminal disorder.'[8] In this, he was also speaking to an emerging body of Western military thought that saw chaos as a defining characteristic of modern conflicts, even those fought between states. Just as the end of the Cold War made it look unlikely that NATO, and the United States in particular, would be fighting peer rivals – the two Gulf Wars demonstrated the extraordinary impact of Western technological supremacy on the battlefield – the concept of the battlefield itself was changing. The front lines were either deepening or disappearing, depending on how one chose to look at them. In what became called fourth-generation warfare, the focus would shift from killing enemies to breaking their will to fight, as suited an era in which the West saw itself most likely fighting insurgents or 'insurgent states.'[9] The classic model was a putative – and hybrid – clash with Iran, where the high-technology US Navy might find itself threatened by swarms of speedboats packed with explosives or Revolutionary Guards with anti-tank rockets.

Even before the 'little green men' turned up in Crimea, there was a growing sense that such blended and protean ways of war could also be employed by peer and near-peer states, the dominant side in a conflict, rather than just guerrillas and plucky (or intransigent) underdogs.[10] After all, since 1999 the Chinese had been toying with the notion of so-called 'Unrestricted Warfare' – although Ofer Fridman rightly and usefully notes that a better and less value-laden translation would be 'warfare that transcends boundaries.'[11] The book of that name by Colonels Qiao Liang and Wang Xiangsui presents the familiar notion that old understandings and boundaries of warfare were coming into question, and that success would depend on 'synchrony,' the capacity to fight wars in coordinated simultaneity in a variety of not just physical fronts but also whole domains, from the kinetic to the informational.[12] In what has clear resonances with the Russian approach discussed in future chapters, the Chinese put an emphasis on what they call the 'three warfares' – psychological, informational and legal – to achieve their strategic objectives.

'Between chaos, confusion and Clausewitz'[13]

> Russia has increasingly focused on new and less conventional military techniques. These asymmetric tactics (sometimes described as unconventional, ambiguous or non-linear warfare) techniques [*sic*] are both more aligned to Russian strengths, and considerably more difficult for NATO to counter. The Russian use of asymmetric warfare techniques ... therefore, represents the most immediate threat to its NATO neighbours and other NATO Member States.
>
> (British House of Commons Defence Committee, 2014)[14]

Russia has not redefined the nature of war through its use of proxies, undeclared armies and covert political operations in Crimea and the Donbas, nor yet by twinning this with a campaign of disinformation and political meddling. Although it does cynically cultivate rival extremes abroad, all in the name of spreading chaos and division. In Italy and Greece, for example, it eggs on parties of both left and right (the Five Star Movement and the *Lega*, *Syriza* and Golden Dawn, respectively), not just to make allies but also to generate tensions. Likewise, in its broader narrative it is happy to encourage anti-capitalist and liberal protest movements such as Occupy, as well as to cultivate big business and play to social conservatives.

Any notion that only in the late twentieth century fluid, state, non-state or para-state actors were mixing conventional and unconventional forces and methods as well as espionage, sabotage, criminality, propaganda and subversion is patently untrue. Michael Kofman has drawn imaginative parallels with the *chevauchee* raids that were such a feature of fourteenth-century Europe, but the fact is that the historical examples are ubiquitous.[15] When the thirteenth-century Mongols were rolling across Eurasia, they deliberately spread news of the atrocities they perpetrated on cities that did not surrender and dragged branches behind their horses to raise dust clouds suggesting their armies were far larger than they were, *maskirovka* (deception) and disinformation in one. When privateers – sanctioned pirates – were deployed in conflicts from the medieval campaigns of the Mediterranean to the American Revolutionary War, or when the Allies enlisted the support of the Mafia when invading Sicily in 1943,[16] were these not precursors of Moscow's use of gangsters? One can understand why Russian defence expert Ruslan Pukhov wrote that

> it is obvious that the term 'hybrid warfare' is used as a propaganda device and not really a classification. This is because any attempt to define it ends with the conclusion that there really is nothing very new in the idea.[17]

Each individual aspect of recent operations is familiar, and Moscow maintains a focus on conventional, high-intensity warfighting. Rather, what Russia's recent actions have done is highlight changes in the nature of war that say as much about the evolving battlespace as about Russian military thinking. Thus, the whole hybrid war debate is really two debates intertwined: one about the strategic challenge from an embittered and embattled Russia, and one about the changing nature of war in the modern age.

In the immediate aftermath of the Crimean seizure, though, the notion of a radically new style of hybrid warfighting took the West by storm, and led to both insightful analysis and panicked caricatures.[18] This has been called 'new generation warfare,'[19] 'ambiguous warfare,'[20] 'full-spectrum warfare'[21] or even 'non-linear war,'[22] not least as these are terms with less intellectual baggage associated with them. Robert Seely made a valiant bid to develop a conceptually broad but geographically limited framework with his notion of 'contemporary Russian conflict,' as 'a sophisticated and integrated form of state influence closely linked to political objectives.' He points out that '[i]t has, at its core, the KGB toolkit of "Active Measures,"' which usefully shifts the spotlight from military to political ends, of which more below.[23] For better or (probably) worse, though, hybrid war remains the accepted term of art in Western military and strategic circles. Perhaps, as Latvian scholar Jānis Bērziņš has acidly noted, it has caught on because 'the word hybrid is catchy, since it may represent a mix of anything.'[24]

This tendency has only been encouraged by the emergence of what one could, perhaps rather too belittlingly, call a 'hybrid-industrial complex' of government agencies, think-tanks, non-governmental organisations (NGOs) and pundits whose prominence, relevance and, above all, funds depend on maintaining the drumbeat of alarmist analyses. It has long been a depressing truth that securitising something tends to push it up the political agenda. When refugees become potential terrorists, or when criminals become fifth columnists, then the budgets available to deal with them expand and politicians take greater notice. The hybrid war label, which meant that everything from online disinformation to the flows of dirty Russian money could be considered a precursor to military conflict, became a powerful and contested political instrument.

It is easy to be sanctimonious, of course – not least because the author himself undoubtedly benefited from this moral panic – and it is by no means the case that all or even most of those who threw themselves into the debates about Russian hybrid war were cynical opportunists or clueless followers of fashion. Indeed, this helped bring attention and action to a number of very serious political, security and even ethical concerns. The corruption of Western institutions through dirty money and non-transparent lobbying is a real and present danger to democracy, for example, and even if it took a 'Russia scare' to compel action,[25] then progress in addressing this is surely to be welcomed. Much the same could be true of the debates over the scale and nature of the 'fake news' challenge and how best it can be resisted.

Hybrid war as a security challenge nonetheless

Besides which, whatever one may call it, Russia is mounting a campaign to influence and subvert the West, using everything from aggressive intelligence operations to cultural manipulation. On one level, some argue that it does not matter whether hybrid war exists as a distinct or novel style of contestation, or what we call it. But it matters to get things right. Any effective new policy – both to resist further Russian adventures and also deter other revisionist or aggressive powers from considering this an example to follow – depends on a timely, nuanced and accurate understanding on the strengths and weaknesses of this 'new way of war.'

The risks are, after all, considerable. The current Russian regime appears not only to have staked its political credibility on its revisionist programme,[26] it seems genuinely to believe that this is the only way to preserve Russian sovereignty and cultural integrity. Putin himself speaks increasingly the language of the clash of civilisations between Russia and the West. When justifying the annexation of Crimea, for example, he framed it as a response to a generations-long strategic campaign by the West to isolate and control Russia:

> [W]e have every reason to assume that the infamous policy of containment, led in the eighteenth, nineteenth and twentieth centuries, continues today. They are constantly trying to sweep us into a corner because we have an independent position, because we maintain it and because we call things like they are and do not engage in hypocrisy.[27]

This atmosphere of tension and confrontation is thus likely to continue, regardless of the outcomes of the current struggle in Ukraine.[28] On the one hand, an over-reaction will play to Putin's narrative of grievance. It may also force the Kremlin into more overt aggression in its neighbourhood and mischief-making beyond it. On the other hand, under-reaction could encourage further adventures, just as the unexpected ease of the seizure of Crimea helped make the case in Moscow for further moves in Ukraine. It may also embolden and inform other revisionist states that may see in Russia's techniques a blueprint for their own destabilising adventures.

So, this is why it matters to understand the phenomenon we are calling hybrid war, and to appreciate that it only truly can be said to apply to a proportion, a fraction, of Russia's wider challenge, and, as will be explored below, why it is best considered through the lens of political warfare. To deter and resist Russia most effectively, it must be understood, shorn of the temptations to exaggerate, demonise and mobilise the threat for political purpose. In comprehension there is the best security: to flip an increasingly over-used cliché, this is the true weaponisation of information.

Notes

1 Guillaume Lasconjarias and Jeffrey Larsen (eds), *NATO's Response to Hybrid Threats* (NATO Defense College, 2015), p. xxi.

2 International Institute for Strategic Studies, *Military Balance 2015*, editor's introduction www.iiss.org/en/publications/military%20balance/issues/the-military-balance-2015-5ea6/mb2015-00b-foreword-eff4. All websites cited in this book were last accessed on 17 December 2018.

3 See, for example, Frank Hoffman, 'On not-so-new warfare: political warfare vs hybrid threats,' War on the Rocks, 28 July 2014 https://warontherocks.com/2014/07/on-not-so-new-warfare-political-warfare-vs-hybrid-threats/.

4 MCDC Countering Hybrid Warfare Project, *Understanding Hybrid Warfare* (MCDC, 2017), p. 3.

5 Speaking at his confirmation hearings before the Senate Armed Services Committee. He also noted: '[If] you want to talk about a nation that could pose an existential threat to the United States, I'd have to point to Russia.' *New York Times*, 9 July 2015.

6 Though, of course, there are limits to such direct comparisons, as the Russian military gets rather more bang for its ruble.

7 Conversation, Norfolk VA, March 2016.

8 Frank Hoffman, *Conflict in the Twenty-first Century: the Rise of Hybrid Warfare* (Potomac Institute, 2000), p. 14.

9 Simplistically put, first-generation warfare was that fought by the massed armies of the ancient and medieval world; muskets and rifles ushered in

second-generation warfare, where the emphasis was on manoeuvring smaller forces into positions where they could be most effective; third-generation warfare, heralded by the German *blitzkrieg* of the Second World War, was shaped by fast, hard-striking armoured units with air support to break through enemy lines. Fourth-generation warfare sees the battlespace expanded to all available networks, whether military or political, economic or social, to deter the potential enemy or demonstrate that the cost of achieving their ends is too great.

10 See, for example, Michael Breen and Joshua Geltzer, 'Asymmetric strategies as strategies of the strong,' *Parameters*, Spring 2011.

11 Ofer Fridman, *Russian 'Hybrid Warfare'* (Hurst, 2018), p. 12.

12 Released in translation as Qiao Liang and Wang Xiangsui, *Unrestricted Warfare* (Pan-American Publishing Company, 2002).

13 This term was used by a participant at a 2015 NATO Allied Command Transformation conference; see Enrico Fassi, Sonia Lucarelli and Alessandro Marrone (eds), *What NATO – for What Threats? Warsaw and Beyond* (NATO, 2015), p. 10.

14 UK House of Commons Defence Committee, 'Towards the next defence and security review: part two – NATO,' *Third Report of Session 2014–5, HC358* (2015) www.publications.parliament.uk/pa/cm201415/cmselect/cmdfence/358/35805.htm.

15 Michael Kofman, 'Raiding and international brigandry: Russia's strategy for great power competition,' War on the Rocks, 14 June 2018 https://warontherocks.com/2018/06/raiding-and-international-brigandry-russias-strategy-for-great-power-competition/.

16 The facts of such a deal have been hotly debated, but the evidence suggests an understanding, one that allowed a Mafia that had been hard-pressed to re-establish itself in Sicily. For contrasting views, see Salvatore Lupo, 'The Allies and the Mafia,' *Journal of Modern Italian Studies*, 2, 1 (1997) and Ezio Costanzo, *The Mafia and the Allies* (Enigma, 2007).

17 Ruslan Pukhov, 'Mif o "gibridnoi voine",' *Nezavisimoe voennoe obozrenie*, 29 May 2015.

18 For an interesting discussion, see Bettina Renz, 'Russia and "hybrid warfare",' *Contemporary Politics*, 22, 3 (2016), pp. 283–300. Ofer Fridman's *Russian 'Hybrid Warfare'* (Hurst, 2018) is the pick of the current literature on this debate.

19 See, for example, Martin Murphy, 'Understanding Russia's concept for total war in Europe,' *Heritage Foundation Special Report 184*, 9 September 2016.

20 See, for example, *Russia's "Ambiguous Warfare" and Implications for the U.S. Marine Corps*, CNA, May 2015 www.cna.org/CNA_files/PDF/DOP-2015-U-010447-Final.pdf.

21 Usefully summarised in this context in Oscar Jonsson and Robert Seely, 'Russian full-spectrum conflict: an appraisal after Ukraine,' *Journal of Slavic Military Studies*, 28, 1 (2015) pp. 1–22.

22 This term was prominent in a story written by Vladislav Surkov, Putin's former political technologist. See Peter Pomerantsev, 'How Putin is reinventing warfare,' *Foreign Policy*, 5 May 2014 and Mark Galeotti, 'Putin's secret weapon,' *Foreign Policy*, 7 July 2014.

23 Robert Seely, *A Definition of Contemporary Russian Conflict: How Does the Kremlin Wage War?* (Henry Jackson Society, 2018), p. 2. Active measures, which will be discussed below, are covert political operations.

24 Jānis Bērziņš, 'Russian new generation warfare is not hybrid warfare,' in Artis Pabriks and Andis Kudors (eds), *The War in Ukraine: Lessons for Europe* (University of Latvia Press, 2015), p. 43.

25 A particularly trenchant take is Oliver Bullough, *Moneyland: Why Thieves and Crooks Now Rule the World and How to Take It Back* (Profile, 2018).

26 See Dmitri Trenin, 'Russia's breakout from the post-Cold War system: the drivers of Putin's course,' *Carnegie Moscow Center*, 22 December 2014.

27 'Address by President of the Russian Federation,' 18 March 2014 http://en.special.kremlin.ru/events/president/news/20603.

28 For an excellent analysis, see András Rácz, *Russia's Hybrid War in Ukraine* (Finnish Institute of International Affairs, 2015).

2 The roots of Russian conduct

> The problem you Americans have in dealing with us is that you think
> you understand us, but you don't. You look at the Chinese and you
> think: 'They're not like us.' You look at us Russians, and you think,
> 'They're like us.' But you're wrong. We are not like you.
>
> (Quote attributed to Vladimir Putin)[1]

The debate as to whether Russians are Europeans, Asians, Eurasians
or something else is centuries old and still running. Nonetheless, when
it comes to security policy, it is clear that Moscow has distinctive
concerns, ways of looking at the world, and notions as to how to
respond to perceived threats. While some of the intellectual debates
will be covered later, it is worth first dwelling on quite why the Kremlin
became convinced that it was facing an existential cultural and political struggle with the West and responded the way it did. To a degree,
this relates to the mismatch between its self-image and the way it was
treated by the West – essentially, the United States – but also the terms
of Putin's efforts to restore Russia to what he considers its rightful place,
and the gap between Putin's aspirations and the country's actual capacities. In that context, this also reflects the institutional context, the
progressive personalisation of politics under first Boris Yeltsin, then
Vladimir Putin, which encourages an essentially entrepreneurial and
disruptive model of politics.

Beaten down

> Some argue that there are no external threats to Russia, beyond
> terrorism or internal conflicts. That defence expenditures are too high.
> That the notion of the defence of the Fatherland and compulsory mili-
> tary service have lost their meaning ... However, the fact is that the

security threats to Russia are not only not disappearing, but increasing ever more.

(General Makhmut Gareev, 2013)[2]

A recurring theme in Russian official and unofficial statements is the belief that their country has been belittled and beaten down by the West. In March 2014, even as Moscow was consolidating its grip on Crimea and inserting itself into the Donbas, US president Barack Obama infamously described Russia as 'a regional power that is threatening some of its immediate neighbours – not out of strength but out of weakness.'[3] While in many ways objectively true, this apparently infuriated Putin, who bristled, calling the claim 'disrespectful' and downright wrong.[4] In part, this anger was likely simply a symptom of the wider collapse in Russian-Western relations, the product of a new conviction that Russia was not only betrayed in the past, but also it is at threat today.

Having come to power in 2000 essentially as a pragmatic nationalist, sceptical of Western values and aims, but accepting that Russia's future lay in greater economic and political cooperation with it, even before his return to the presidency in 2012, Putin appears to have changed.[5] Increasingly he appears to believe his own rhetoric and, indeed, his own mythology, demonstrating a personal and ideological shift towards a more aggressive Russian nationalism. His expressed view is that Russia's place in the world and its distinctive and irreplaceable culture are being threatened and actively undermined by Western values and political ambitions. As he put it in 2011, 'sometimes it seems to me that America does not need allies, it needs vassals.'[6]

There is not the room here to go through the full Kremlin litany of Western perfidies, from 'betrayal' over NATO expansion, through 'organising the colour revolutions of Ukraine, Georgia and Kyrgyzstan,' to 'sponsoring' anti-corruption and pro-democracy activism and opposition movements in Russia itself. That would take a book in its own right.[7] Some have a certain justice about them, others patently not. What is important here is that this is not simply a convenient political narrative to demonise the opposition and mobilise nationalist sentiments – although it undoubtedly is both – but it is also a genuinely held view within a significant fraction of the political and especially security elite, most notably Vladimir Putin and his closest allies.

Security Council Secretary Nikolai Patrushev, for example, has bluntly asserted that the USA 'would very much like Russia not to exist at all – as a country.'[8] Former State Duma speaker and now head of the Foreign Intelligence Service (SVR) Sergei Naryshkin has an even more florid take, claiming that 'Washington seeks instability … to continue old and launch new acts of assault and plunder' as it stirs 'up anti-Russian sentiments in Europe.'[9] Putin himself has claimed:

> Our western partners, led by the United States of America, prefer not to be guided by international law in their practical policies, but by the rule of the gun. They have come to believe in their exclusivity and exceptionalism, that they can decide the destinies of the world, that only they can ever be right.[10]

This has also become a self-sustaining process. Given the Kremlin's especially broad sense of quite what constitutes 'war,' for example, the very measures imposed by the West in order to try and bring home condemnation of Russian aggression, economic sanctions, are themselves considered unilaterally hostile acts. When Andrei Kostin, chair of state-owned VTB Bank, affirmed that 'sanctions, in other words, are economic war against Russia,' he was speaking for the Kremlin.[11]

Moscow genuinely believes it is working to try and catch up in developing state-wrecking and coercive capabilities acquired and honed by the West. However wrong-headed it may be, this perception shapes the Russian approach to hybrid war and the ways it is building its own capabilities. Consider, for example, a speech given by Chief of the General Staff General Valerii Gerasimov in 2016:

> It is necessary to focus on the main components of [Western] hybrid methods. The falsification of events, control of the media are among the most effective methods of asymmetric warfare. The effect can be comparable with the results of large-scale use of troops and forces.
>
> Illustrative examples are the incitement of nationalism in Ukraine, the revolutionary unrest in the Arab world. The massive impact on the minds of people contributed to the growth of the protest potential of the population, and the spread of 'colour movements' in the states of North Africa, which led to a change of political regimes in some of them.[12]

Hence the belief that *gibridnaya voina* is a quintessentially American invention, drawing on Western economic and soft power to bring about political change through covert and deniable means.[13] This not only contributes to a sense of being under constant threat – and from a covert and subtle threat that could be behind any reversal, from labour unrest to lost trade opportunities – but it also provides a justification for Russia's own campaigns.

Making Russia great again

> Russia has been a great power for centuries, and remains so. It has always had and still has legitimate zones of interest … We should not drop our guard in this respect, neither should we allow our opinion to be ignored.
>
> (Vladimir Putin, 1999)[14]

Putin's Russia is strong on ambitions, weak on resources. From this mismatch comes a great deal of ingenuity, improvisation and introspection, as well as – in a pattern visible over the centuries – a justification for tight central control, to allow a concentration of resources on national security.[15] After all, it is seeking not only to maintain a significant global status as a great power, whose voice must be heard on all important matters, but it also has specific aspirations towards maintaining a sphere of influence in post-Soviet Eurasia (with the apparent exception of the Baltic States, which are generally accepted as having been 'lost'[16]). It must do that, though, under sharp limitations.

In the final analysis, most power is directly or indirectly economic in nature. Admittedly, an authoritarian regime is much more able to focus resources on its strategic priorities. Russia, for example, officially devotes around 4% of its gross domestic product (GDP) to defence, although deeper analysis suggests the real figure is closer to 6%, compared with a European NATO average of 1.2%.[17] Nonetheless, it is still constrained by the overall size of its economy, whose sluggish performance has forced the Kremlin to shrink the defence budget since 2016.[18] This inevitably affects military strength directly and indirectly, from eating into procurement and training programmes to making it harder to pay the salaries and provide the living conditions needed to attract and retain good personnel. Despite a clear Kremlin commitment to defence-related research and development for both domestic use and export opportunities, economic weaknesses and poor past investment decisions have also served to undermine Russia's technological capacities at a time when the nature of war is being reshaped by rapid (and expensive) advances.

In fairness, the newest kit tomorrow is less useful than adequate kit today, and Russia's capacities should not be discounted. Furthermore, in classic Russian style, ingenuity has gone into leveraging what partial strengths it has, such as turning to hackers to address gaps in cyber capabilities. However, these are stopgap measures and cannot conceal – not least from its own military planners – a widening technology gap with the United States and, perhaps even more shocking to Moscow, the loss of a long-assumed advantage over China.[19]

Beyond that, there is considerable debate as to the Russian population's long-term trends. The consensus appears to be that a crisis is looming. The 2010 census registered a population drop of almost 3% in the past eight years, to 142.9 million, and a 2015 report from the Russian Presidential Academy of National Economy and Public Administration suggested it could be down 20%, to 113 million by 2050.[20] This has all kinds of implications, from the lack of potential conscripts and young, able-bodied workers, through to the need to encourage migration from China and Central Asia, which to many in the government poses security and geopolitical risks in its own right.

Finally, in the modern world, cultural capital and economic weight are powerful instruments of geopolitics. A hydrocarbon state is hostage to vicissitudes in oil and gas prices, and Putin's previously touted successes of the 2000s were largely a matter of simple good luck and high prices. Russia's soft power is limited, its image in the world distinctly lacklustre. The Pew Research Centre's 2017 survey of world opinion found only 34% of respondents viewing Russia positively: only in Vietnam, Greece and the Philippines were half or more of the population favourable towards it.[21] Some dictators may appreciate Putin's triumphs, some would-be strongmen see him as a figure to copy. There are social conservatives who believe Russia is a bulwark against changing values, and others who see it as a counterweight to American global dominance. But in the main, Russia is not considered a rising power, or a model to emulate. It is telling, for example, that the only countries Moscow could persuade to recognise its annexation of Crimea were Afghanistan, Cuba, Kyrgyzstan, Nicaragua, North Korea, Syria and Venezuela.

Guerrilla geopolitics

> If we confine ourselves to the West's model of diplomacy, we are letting them choose the game and pick the teams.
> (Russian Ministry of Foreign Affairs official, 2016)[22]

Put all these elements together and Russia's claims to great-power status and its scope to assert the kind of global role Putin claims begin to look threadbare. It has nuclear weapons, to be sure, but these are tools of limited utility. They may be used in heavy-handed intimidation, such as the threat made to Poland in 2008 that if it went ahead with basing US anti-missile systems, it was 'making itself a target. This is 100% certain.'[23] They may also be used, conceivably, in a limited, tactical attack to 'de-escalate' a conventional war – in other words, to bring it to an end on terms favourable to Russia. The former does not seem very effective, though, and the latter extremely risky. One General Staff officer dismissed the 'escalate to de-escalate' notion as 'the kind of idea dreamed up by theoreticians, not practical'[24] and the balance of evidence is that no such doctrine exists.[25]

Instead, Russia is left with a military force that is still only – permanently – part-way through modernisation, a process coming under growing economic pressure. Its armed forces number some million uniformed personnel, but the crucial ground forces only represent around a third of that.[26] Around half of these are conscripts, banned by law from being sent into combat other than in times of formal war, and serving terms of just one year, scarcely enough to train them properly and meaning they are only truly operational for perhaps three–four months of that year. Given that, according to Ukrainian accounts, at least 40,000 and often more are typically stationed in Crimea and in and near the Donbas, that others need to be based in the turbulent North Caucasus, and that more are scattered along Russia's lengthy border, this is not as many as it may sound, especially given the need to rotate forces that have seen action.

This is by no means a negligible force, especially for post-Soviet neighbours lacking the protections of NATO membership. Even after two years of reform and rearmament, Ukraine's entire military establishment numbered 210,000 soldiers and 40,000 civilians, for example, while Georgia by contrast had but 37,000.[27] Nonetheless, Putin's apparent aspirations are not simply to be a limited regional power able to bully smaller and poorer neighbours. Rather, the intent, however optimistic, is to be able to assert a meaningful global role.

The answer could be characterised as 'guerrilla geopolitics.' Why, as the Russian diplomat argued in the quote opening this section, stick to rules that favour the opposition? Like any smart insurgent, Russia seeks to avoid conflict where it is weak and its enemies strong, but rather to shift the battle to terrain of its own choosing. To a large extent this means politics, taking advantage of the fact that an authoritarian state can generally be more ruthless, risk-taking, unpredictable and disciplined than a constellation of democracies with their own internal debates and divisions. In this context, the military notion of hybrid war is an attempt to make limited forces go further, degrading the defensive capacities of an enemy before the actual fighting. In Crimea, breaking their chain of command, disrupting military morale and creating temporary uncertainty as to quite what was going on meant the Ukrainian soldiers on the peninsula simply needed to be penned, captured and expelled, not fought to a defeat. Likewise, political war is a substitute for having to deploy those overstretched elite forces and the under-reformed rest of the military, especially against an enemy such as NATO. Rather it bypasses most of these objective weaknesses of Russia's and instead capitalises on the enemy's subjective ones. The West, after all, fears much: it fears social disruption and expensive foreign commitments; it fears being manipulated by its own media and let down by the complex systems on which it relies; it fears ambitious rising competitors and embittered old antagonists. By gamesmanship, corruption and disinformation instead of direct force, Moscow seems to mobilise and direct those fears to induce the West to see Russia as too disruptive and inconvenient an antagonist to be worth challenging. Paraphrasing Franklin D. Roosevelt, one might suggest that Russia has nothing to use, but fear itself. The more the West builds up the scale and power of the Kremlin 'threat,' the more it empowers it and creates a self-fulfiling prophecy, as this encourages the Russians to do something with that power.

Hybrid war for a hybrid state

> [W]hat distinguishes the current Russian government from the erstwhile Soviet leaders familiar to the West is its rejection of ideological constraints and the complete elimination of institutions.
> (Russian oligarch-turned-dissident Mikhail Khodorkovskii)[28]

Moscow's approach also reflects the political character of Putin's Russia. One distinctive aspect of its recent campaigns, from political ones against the West to military ones in Ukraine, has been a blurring of the borders between state, para-state, mercenary and dupe. The importance of national mobilisation, discussed below, extends to mining society as a whole for semi-autonomous assets, whether eager internet trolls and 'patriotic hackers,' or Cossack volunteers and gangsters.

William Nemeth used the term hybrid war in connection with Russia's war in Chechnya,[29] essentially in the context of kinetic struggles in which terrorism and even pseudo-criminal operations are used to support more conventional assets. This was rooted in his belief that Chechen society was itself a hybrid, still somewhere between the modern and the pre-modern, where traditional forms of social organisation, notably the family and the *teip* (clan) could be used to mobilise for war in ways that need not or would not distinguish between 'regular' and 'irregular' forms of war. Hence, a hybrid society fought a hybrid war.

The 'hybridity' of Russian operations reflects a conceptually analogous, even if operationally very different, 'hybridity' of the Russian state.

Through the 1990s and into Putinism, it has, however you choose to define it, either failed to institutionalise or actively deinstitutionalised. This is a patrimonial, hyper-presidential regime characterised by the permeability of boundaries between public and private, domestic and external. Lacking meaningful rule of law or checks and balances, without drawing too heavy-handed a comparison with fascism, Putin's Russia seems implicitly to embody, in its own way, Mussolini's dictum '*tutto nello Stato, niente al di fuori dello Stato, nulla contro lo Stato*' (everything inside the state, nothing outside the state, nothing against the state).[30]

State institutions are often regarded as personal fiefdoms and piggy banks, and officials and even officers freely engage in commercial activity. The media – especially TV – are not just a tool of official propaganda but also of personal rivalry. The Russian Orthodox Church is practically an arm of the Kremlin. The police and security services are economic actors as well as government agencies. The legislature is largely a sock-puppet institution. While private business and civil society exist, and in some cases thrive, they are also expected to operate as Kremlin assets as and when required. Not just *nulla contro lo Stato*, but *tutto per lo Stato* (everything for the state). In such an environment, the infusion of non-military instruments into military affairs was almost inevitable.

This is essentially an 'adhocracy,' in which the true elite is defined by service to the needs of the Kremlin rather than any specific institutional or social identity. They may be spies, diplomats, journalists, politicians or millionaires; essentially they are all 'political entrepreneurs' who must seek to serve the Kremlin or are required to do so, often regardless of their formal role.[31] As a result, Putin's Russia is characterised by multiple, overlapping agencies, a 'bureaucratic pluralism' intended as much to permit the Kremlin to divide and rule as for any practical advantages. Of course, this entrepreneurialism cuts both ways. Everyone – nearly everyone – exploits their position for personal gain. Internal competition can be deeply dysfunctional, and the state more easily be hijacked for personal and factional advantage. Regardless, though, this is the model in place. Moscow does not chose to ignore those boundaries we are used to in the West between state and private, military and civilian, legal and illegal. It is rather that those boundaries are simply much less meaningful in Russian terms, and additionally straddled by a range of duplicative and even competitive agencies. This can get in the way of coherent policy and create problems of redundancy and even contradictory goals, such as the 2016 US electoral hack, where FSB (Federal Security Service) and GRU (Main Intelligence Directorate) operations appear to have been working at cross purposes.[32] However, it also creates a challenge that is complex, multi-faceted and inevitably difficult for Western agencies to comprehend, let alone counter.

Notes

1 Fiona Hill and Clifford Gaddy, 'The American education of Vladimir Putin,' *The Atlantic*, 16 February 2015.
2 Makhmut Gareev, 'Na "myagkuyu silu" naidutsya zhestkie otvety,' *Voenno-promyshlenny kur'er*, 4 December 2013.
3 *Guardian*, 25 March 2014.
4 In an interview with the German newspaper *Bild*, 12 January 2016.
5 Mark Galeotti and Andrew Bowen, 'Putin's empire of the mind,' *Foreign Policy*, 21 April 2014.
6 *Daily Telegraph*, 15 December 2011.
7 For especially useful examples, see Peter Conradi, *Who Lost Russia?: How the World Entered a New Cold War* (OneWorld, 2017); Richard Sakwa, *Russia Against the Rest: The Post-Cold War Crisis of World Order* (Cambridge University Press, 2017); and Shaun Walker, *The Long Hangover: Putin's New Russia and the Ghosts of the Past* (Oxford University Press USA, 2018).
8 *Kommersant*, 22 June 2015.
9 *Rossiskaya gazeta*, 9 August 2015.
10 'Address by President of the Russian Federation,' 18 March 2014 http://en.special.kremlin.ru/events/president/news/20603.
11 CNBC, 30 January 2015.
12 In a speech to the annual general meeting of the Academy of Military Sciences, 27 February 2016; his speech was reproduced in *Voenno-promyshlenny kur'er*, 9 March 2016.
13 There is a depressingly rich body of Russian writing, from serious military analysis to extreme conspiracy theory, on this supposed struggle, including Sergei Tkachenko, *Informatsionnaya voina protiv Rossii* (Piter, 2011); Mikhail Zakharov, 'Boitsy gibridnogo fronta,' *Mir i politika*, June 2014; Sergei Glaziev, 'O vneshnikh i vnutrennikh ugrozakh ekonomicheskoi bezopasnosti Rossii v uslovyakh amerikanskoi agressii,' *Menedzhment i biznes-administrirovanie zhurnal* 2 (2015); A. Manoilo, 'Gibridnye voiny I tsverye revolyutsii v mirovoi politike,' *Pravo i politika*, 7/2015; V. A. Nagornyi, 'Sobytye na yugo-vostoke Ukrainy v kontekste kontseptsii "gibridnykh voin",' *Panorama* 20 (2015); V. A. Kiselev and I. N. Vorob'ev, 'Gibridnye operatsii kak novyi vid voennogo protivoborstva,' *Voennaya mysl'*, 24, 5 (2015).
14 Speech to the State Duma, quoted in BBC, 28 March 2014.
15 This is a theme which was best expanded upon by Richard Pipes, notably in his *Russia under the Old Regime* (Weidenfeld & Nicolson, 1974).
16 A phrase that cropped up independently in several conversations with Russian diplomatic and military interlocutors.
17 Paul Gregory, 'Russia cooks its defense books,' *Politico*, 17 November 2015.

18 Reuters, 6 March 2016; Bloomberg, 12 September 2016.

19 It is worth noting that for all Moscow and Beijing may talk of strategic partnership and mount joint exercises – not least to unnerve Washington – the Russians still update their contingency plans for war with China on an annual basis.

20 Ilan Berman, 'Russia's fraught demographic future,' *Jamestown Foundation Russia in Decline Project*, 13 September 2016.

21 Pew Research Center, 2017 Global Indicators Database, 'Opinion of Russia.'

22 Conversation, Moscow, February 2016.

23 Interfax, 15 August 2008.

24 Conversation, Moscow, April 2014.

25 Olga Oliker, 'Russia's nuclear doctrine: what we know, what we don't, and what that means,' CSIS, May 2016.

26 The size at the start of 2018 was fixed at 1,013,628. TASS, 1 January 2018.

27 Ukrainian Ministry of Defence, *White Book 2015* www.mil.gov.ua/content/files/whitebook/WB_2015_eng_WEB.PDF; Georgi Tskhvitava, 'Boost to military reform in Georgia,' IWPR, 19 July 2016 https://iwpr.net/global-voices/boost-military-reform-georgia.

28 Mikhail Khodorkovsky, 'Plan for life after Putin,' *Politico*, 10 June 2016.

29 In his 2002 Master's thesis 'Future war and Chechnya: a case for hybrid warfare' at the Naval Postgraduate School, Monterey, CA http://calhoun.nps.edu/bitstream/handle/10945/5865/02Jun_Nemeth.pdf?sequence=1.

30 As a point of interest, Mussolini sent what could be called 'little black-shirt men' to Spain in 1936–1939 to fight on Franco's side during the civil war, notionally all volunteers (as the Voluntary Troops Corps) and initially without insignia.

31 I explore this further in 'Russia has no grand plans, but lots of "adhocrats",' *Business New Europe*, 18 January 2017 www.intellinews.com/stolypin-russia-has-no-grand-plans-but-lots-of-adhocrats-114014/.

32 Dmitri Alperovich, 'Bears in the midst: intrusion into the Democratic National Committee,' CrowdStrike, 15 June 2016 www.crowdstrike.com/blog/bears-midst-intrusion-democratic-national-committee/; Thomas Rid, 'All signs point to Russia being behind the DNC hack,' Motherboard, 25 July 2016 https://motherboard.vice.com/en_us/article/4xa5g9/all-signs-point-to-russia-being-behind-the-dnc-hack.

3   The view from the Kremlin

We may not accept that the West has tried to engineer regime change in North Africa, the Middle East and Eurasia, that it is committed to hobbling Russia, or that its commitments to the spread of democracy and transparency are hypocrisies, sanctimonious platitudes weaponised for national gain. But so long as the Kremlin sincerely does, then these beliefs will shape its doctrines and policies. In Ken Booth's words:

> Unless we attempt to understand the character of different cultures it will be impossible to appreciate the mainsprings of National Strategies. Without knowing about the pride, prestige or prejudice, moral outrage, insistence on survival, vanity, vengeance of different societies how can we begin to appreciate the roles, which such important peoples ... might play in contemporary and future military problems?[1]

Today's Russian thinking is a hybrid itself, between context and concept: what happens when a body of thought that dates back to and through Soviet times meets the demands, opportunities and idiosyncrasies of the modern world. This chapter will therefore look not so much on the political agendas and dilemmas of the present as the intellectual antecedents and debates of current thinking.

The mythological Gerasimov Doctrine

The Russians certainly believe the nature of war is changing, and in ways that mean the use of direct force may not always or initially be a central element of the conflict. In 2013, Chief of the General Staff Valerii Gerasimov wrote:

The role of non-military means of achieving political and strategic goals has grown, and, in many cases, they have exceeded the power of force of weapons in their effectiveness … The focus of applied methods of conflict has altered in the direction of the broad use of political, economic, informational, humanitarian, and other non-military measures—applied in coordination with the protest potential of the population. All this is supplemented by military means of a concealed character, including carrying out actions of informational conflict and the actions of special-operations forces. The open use of forces—often under the guise of peacekeeping and crisis regulation—is resorted to only at a certain stage, primarily for the achievement of final success in the conflict.[2]

Gerasimov was not presenting a blueprint for a future without conventional military operations, nor yet hybrid war as understood in the West. Instead, he was expressing Russia's conviction that the modern world was seeing more complex and politically-led forms of contestation alongside regular warfare. To this end, as will be explored below, Russia's supposed 'new way of war' can be considered simply a recognition of the age-old truth that the political has primacy over the kinetic – and that if one side can disrupt the others' will and ability to resist, then the actual strength of their military forces becomes much less relevant, even if not necessarily redundant.

However, this article, written by a tough and competent tank officer whose track record shows no particular interest in, or flair for, military theory, and issued in an obscure publication at that (*Voenno-promyshlennyi kur'er*, the *Military-Industrial Courier*), became taken by many precisely as a 'framework for the new operational concept,' with Gerasimov hailed as a 'the architect of Russia's asymmetrical warfare.'[3] Before long, there was talk of a 'Gerasimov Doctrine,' even though this is entirely mythical. US Senator Chris Coons wrote that Russia 'enthusiastically—and, so far, somewhat successfully—employed the Gerasimov Doctrine by waging a covert and undeclared hybrid war on the West.'[4] Even the US Army's Asymmetric Warfare Group's *Russian New Generation Warfare Handbook* uses the term.[5]

Yet there is no such doctrine. I feel comfortable asserting this as, to my shame, I actually originated the phrase, although it was certainly not intended as a serious term of art. This was Gerasimov's take on events in North Africa (especially Libya, where Putin was furious that Moscow's agreement for a limited United Nations response was, in his eyes, abused to allow an all-out exercise in regime change) and then Syria. I used the term as a throw-away line to spice up the title of a blog post.[6] Having warned in the text that it was not a doctrine as such, and that this formulation was simply a placeholder for the ideas evolving in Russian military thinking, I thought no more about it. This proved to be a serious error: a snappy phrase that spoke to deep-seated Western fears of a 'hybrid gap' – to paraphrase both the Cold War's 'missile gap' and *Dr Strangelove*'s 'mine gap' – as well as a concern that war was outgrowing old paradigms, created a myth that overshadowed the reality.[7]

Taken in the round, Gerasimov's article – which was an encapsulation of previous debates more than a novel exegesis – presented hybrid war (without using the term) not as an end in itself, but as a stage that could or would lead to chaos and the emergence of fierce armed civil conflict into which foreign countries could inject themselves – and that Russia itself was potentially vulnerable.[8] His aim was to be able to have the kind of forces able to shut out such external intervention and fight and quickly win any conflicts, using massive and precise military force. Of course, Russia – like all nations – was not above using non-military tactics to prepare the battlefield, as discussed below. But in so far as there was anything new in that article, it was of his outlining a vision that was in many ways an essentially defensive one for a chaotic modern era, not of an army of covert saboteurs but rather a high-readiness force able rapidly to mobilise and focus firepower on direct, conventional threats. In this, he was reprising themes that had emerged in much recent military theoretical literature and presenting a sense of the comprehensive threats facing Russia, threats that required an equally comprehensive answer.[9] After all, as Andrew Monaghan has perceptively observed, facing what appears to be a near-term future of unpredictability and instability, the Russian state has adopted a strategy of mobilisation involving 'what are in effect efforts to move the country on to a permanent war footing.'[10]

It also reflected the political needs of the moment. Having seen revolutions topple or shake friendly regimes in Africa, the Middle East and even post-Soviet Eurasia, the Kremlin itself was getting worried about *gibridnaya voina*. The Chief of the General Staff is not just a military manager, but he is also by definition a bureaucratic advocate. His article was part of a campaign to prove to a leadership suddenly more worried about political threats that they were also military ones that the armed forces had a plan to respond, and a credible claim for its funding. Admittedly, there is a long-established trend of discussing offensive strategies and capacities in Aesopian terms, by ascribing them to the other side. However, both Russian military literature and also conversations with Russian military officers and observers underscore the extent to which they truly consider *gibridnaya voina* to be an essentially Western – American – gambit, evident even in their adoption of the direct translation of our term. As one recent retiree who had served in the General Staff's Main Operations Directorate put it: 'we only belatedly came to see the weapon you [Westerners] were developing. Even then, first we thought it just applied in unstable, peripheral countries. Then we saw you could point it at us, too.'[11]

How to square the circle between the lack of any serious Russian thinking and writing about *gibridnaya voina* except relatively recently and in the context primarily of Western operations, and the apparent observable distinctiveness of much Russian activity? Is this another piece of *maskirovka* (deception), whereby Moscow was somehow able to keep an evolving military debate hidden? Hardly, not least because for it to be meaningfully applicable to the Russian military it needs to be discussed and manifested in everything from training programmes to procurement plans. Rather, what has been interpreted as something qualitatively new is instead the product of the Russians' take on the way changes in the world are influencing warfare, mediated through their own particular political, historical and cultural prisms.

Moving the battlefield

So if Gerasimov was not inking out some dramatic new chapter in Russian military thought, what are the intellectual antecedents of current thinking? Much is reminiscent of Western debates, especially as soldier-scholars grapple with changing technological and political contexts. As in so many other ways, the tone was set by General Makhmut Gareev, former Deputy Chief of the General Staff, then president of the Russian Academy of Military Sciences, and still dean of the country's military theoreticians. In 2013, he wrote:

> Nations have always struggled with one another with the use of armed forces and warfare capabilities, including intelligence and counterintelligence, deception and stratagems, disinformation, and all other refined and devious stratagems the adversaries could think up. It has always been held that any confrontation without resort to arms is struggle and pursuit of policies by physical force and armed violence is war. Some of our ... philosophers, though, maintain that all non-military practices are a contemporary development and suggest, on this assumption, that following these practices is nothing short of war.[12]

A century-old debate in Russian theoretical circles about the definition of war in many ways echoes Hoffman in his identification of organised armed state violence as the crucial factor distinguishing 'struggle' from 'war.' Time and again, military writers flirted with the notion of war without open fighting. Back in 1997, for example, V. P. Gulin used the study of information war to suggest that in the modern era, social violence – which could include political struggle – could be considered akin to true war.[13] Interestingly it was Colonel Vladimir Kvachkov, a controversial ultra-nationalist special forces officer later convicted of attempting to stage a coup, who, in 2004, pushed beyond orthodoxy to suggest that it might actually be worth formally distinguishing between 'war with the use of armed warfare' and 'war with non-military means,' in effect raising the very division between hybrid/regular and political war that has come to dominate Russian strategy.[14] Nonetheless, the official line remained that war meant war, that it was the domain of the armed forces, even in the post-Ukraine era. Colonel Sergei Chekinov, head of the General Staff's Centre for Military Strategic Studies, and his colleague Lieutenant General Sergei Bogdanov, for example, two more stars of the theoretical firmament, asserted:

> If armed struggle and other actions by armed forces dominate how political objectives are achieved, while all other non-military forms of violence are bent to maximising the effect of using armed forces, this is none other than war. Acting on this premise, political confrontation is not war if the focus is on non-military forms of violence, where the effect of armed forces is due merely to their presence or some action … confined to demonstrations, threats, etc.[15]

This has, after all, long been the official military line. Indeed, the magisterial Soviet *Marksism-Leninism o voine i armii* (*Marxism-Leninism on War and the Army*) concluded that 'the essence of war is the continuation of politics by armed force.'[16] However, even in Soviet times, while not challenging the military's ontology, in practice the political leadership held a much more fluid and comprehensive concept of warfighting. The Kremlin's incumbents then, as today, saw wholly non-military yet essentially assertive and subversive approaches as interchangeable with directly military ones. The military was expected – and did – to adapt to its needs and priorities, just as Gerasimov's statement was in many ways an attempt to bridge the gap between the soldiers and their political masters.

Steering a path between rejecting and too easily accepting the notion of war by non-military means has been eased not only by the realities of the post-Soviet balance of power but also a keen awareness of the potentially revolutionary impact of advanced long-range systems. From the smart missiles able to sink aircraft carriers and blast command centres to the computer-guided electromagnetic railguns that could one day claw them from the sky, it is clear technology is creating new weapons of unprecedented range, accuracy and destructiveness. In 2002, for example, the influential military thinker Major General Vladimir Slipchenko suggested that

> any future war will be a non-contact war. It will come from the air and space. Guidance and control will come from space, and the strike will be conducted from the air and from the seas using a large quantity of precision weaponry.[17]

While pouring what resources they could into developing their own high-tech programmes to fight such a 'non-contact war' – with some successes and many more disappointments – the Russians are aware of the technology gap between them and their peer competitors, especially but not only the United States. As one General Staff officer put it, 'we are still living off upgraded legacy systems, and doing it quite well, but God help us when the new-generation systems really start to spread across the world.'[18] However, the guerrilla state looks to compete on its own terms. Non-contact and network-centric warfare[19] depend heavily on communications, on fast but potentially fragile information substructures. Hence Russia's particular interest in using jamming, spoofing and hacking to interfere with the enemy's ability to gather, transmit and use information: if you can't win the game, you change the rules.

Moscow thus had particular reason to look at ways to use political and information operations to capitalise on a perceived Western reluctance to engage in open hostilities and to undermine any will to resist its encroachments. However, this remained a prickly topic for military theorists, and so discussion of Russian – Soviet – experiences in partisan warfare have become in many ways a way of exploring these options safely by parable, without directly tackling the heretical notion of wars without fighting. In Savinkin and Domnin's 2007 collection *Groznoe oruzhie: Malaia voina, partizanstvo i drugie vidy asimmetrichnogo voevaniya v svete naslediya russkikh voennykh mysliteleï* (*Terrible Weapons: Small War, Partisan and Other Types of Asymmetrical Conflict in Light of the Legacy of Russian Military Thinkers*), for example, they explored how states may use guerrilla-like tactics to bring pressure to bear on enemies while maintaining deniability.[20] Such debates can be located in long-standing Russian discussions about the way that the fog of war and the morale on the home front can be weaponised during the prelude to battle. They also draw on a long tradition of Russian interest in emphasising the political dimension of war.

An historic tradition

> Where force is necessary, there it must be applied boldly, decisively and completely. But one must know the limitations of force; one must know when to blend force with a manoeuvre, a blow with an agreement.
>
> (Leon Trotsky)[21]

From the tsars through the Bolsheviks, the Russians have long been accustomed to a style of warfare that refuses to acknowledge any hard and fast distinctions between overt and covert, kinetic and political, and embraces much more eagerly the irregular and the criminal, the spook and the provocateur, the activist and the fellow traveller. Sometimes, this has been out of choice or convenience, but often it has been a response to the usual challenge of seeking to play as powerful an imperial role as possible with only limited resources.

As well as in the experiences of partisan warfare, they have been drawing on discussions about how to fight them. In the West, there has been a habit of treating counter-insurgency and state-to-state warfare as cognate but different. The Russians have long proven more comfortable applying the political lessons of the one to the other. Indeed, their term *malaya voina*, 'small war,' which in literal terms means the same as 'guerrilla,' has a distinctly different sense. It applies to limited and deniable operations by government forces just as much as the activities of insurgents. Under the Bolsheviks, it also acquired a more explicitly political dimension: the division between the government and the generals expected to accomplish the military dimension of its plans was intentionally blurred. The Party did not necessarily expect to have to spell out all the details: the Red Guard, and then the Red Army, was expected to be fully engaged in addressing the ideological intent of national strategy and be aware of the political intent of its actions.

As a result, the Bolsheviks undoubtedly had a relatively modern take on 'small wars.' Although there is literature dating back to the tsarist era,[22] contemporary Russian writings about 'small wars' tend explicitly to trace their pedigree back to early Soviet works such as M. A. Drobov's *Malaya voina: partizanstvo i diversii* (*Small War: Partisan Combat and Diversionary Attacks*) from 1931.[23] The Estonians, after all, rightly note that the Soviets used the same kind of mix of forces as in Crimea – troops without insignia, local proxies and the threat of a full invasion – in a failed but not forgotten operation in 1924.[24] Furthermore, the counter-insurgency approach applied in Central Asia by Lenin's Commission on Turkestan Affairs, *Turkkommissiya*, was in many ways ahead of its time in the integration of military and political operations, government troops, militias, co-opted bandits and covert operators.[25]

Likewise, Soviet military thinkers had been trailblazers in their understanding that warfare was moving beyond the front line and into an enemy's rear. This was central to Mikhail Tukhachevskii's concept of Deep Battle in the 1920s and 1930s, also picked up by his contemporary Georgii Isserson, who argued that past notions of warfare were outdated because 'the neutralisation and attack of the defence were conducted only along the front line of direct combat contact. The defensive depths remained untouched.'[26] Ironically, the most radical thinker along these lines was Evgenii Messner, a tsarist officer who fought against the Bolsheviks and fled Russia in 1920. His outspokenly conservative and anti-Communist writings were banned in Soviet times, but today, when one strips away his jeremiads against the decadence and weakness of liberal societies, his words sound prescient.[27] In 1931, he wrote that

> wars will be comprised not only of the traditional elements of open war, but also the elements of civil war: sabotage, strikes, unrest [and] insurgencies will shake the state's organism … Disputes will undermine the power of the nation and poison [its] soul, making the severe duty of war even more difficult.[28]

More striking still was his prediction, in *Myatezh: imya tret'yey vsemirnoy* (*Subversion: the Name of the Third World War*), that

> [f]uture war will not be fought on the front lines, but throughout the entire territories of both opponents, because behind the front lines, political, social, and economic fronts will appear; they will fight not on a two-dimensional plane, as in olden days, not in a three dimensional space, as has been the case since the birth of military aviation, but in a four-dimensional space, where the psyche of the combatant nations will serve as the fourth dimension.[29]

In the modern world Messner felt instead of a war/peace binary, there were four states: war, half-war, aggressive-diplomacy and diplomacy. He saw *myatezhevoina*, 'subversion war,' defined as 'psychological warfare aimed to conquer the mind and soul of people' as crucial.[30] While Messner's writings were banned in Soviet times, that does not mean they were wholly unknown. They were stored in closed archives and undoubtedly read and considered by senior (and politically vetted) ideological and military thinkers. Colonel General Igor Rodionov, for example, an unabashed Party loyalist and for a while head of the General Staff Academy, had read Messner's work (or perhaps a digest) when he attended the academy in the late 1970s,[31] so these ideas presumably had some traction even then.

After all, Messner was not just writing about how he saw Soviet operations conducted, he was also parallelling behind-the-scenes debates taking place in Moscow. The Soviet military was not only exploring how to strike deep into the enemy rear, but it also maintained a keen interest in political operations, thanks to its aforementioned interest in guerrilla-style operations, and the strong role of both the intelligence services and also the Communist Party's active measures arms.[32] No wonder that Messner's writings have enjoyed a considerable revival in post-Soviet times and been cited and discussed by many of today's foremost military scholars as they grapple with the challenges of modern war.

Information war and active measures

At least Russian military thinkers can also draw on an especially rich experience of information operations, in which many have seen the roots of today's activities.[33] Too much is made of Russia's supposed commitment to 'reflexive control' – described as a means of conditioning an opponent 'voluntarily' to make the decision you want him to make – which is neither unique nor actually central to its planning and operational cycles. Nonetheless, the Soviets were especially concerned with propaganda, misinformation and political manipulation, often with the same goal of masking underlying weaknesses.[34] This tradition also lives on, enriched by the opportunities in the new, diffuse and lightning-speed media age.

Information operations have thus become all the more central to Russian discussions. In the journal *Voennaya mysl'*, Chekinov and Bogdanov noted in 2011 that

> strategic information warfare plays an important role in disrupting military and government leadership and air and space defence systems, misleading the enemy, forming desirable public opinions, organising anti-government activities, and conducting other measures in order to decrease the will of the opponent to resist.[35]

This well describes the military take on information operations, which also has deep historical roots long pre-dating the internet.[36] Western attempts to understand it still too often are based on its own perspectives. To take one specific example, the FSB's 16th Centre and the GRU's 5th Department, believed to be their respective offensive information operations commands, and the FSB's 8th Centre, responsible for information security, all operate in a range of different kinds of activity, from propaganda to direct hacking or even destructive cyberattacks, in defiance of the kind of siloing one would see in the West. This is because 'cyber' as used in the West is not a Russian concept. Rather, the Russians consider information itself, in all its forms, to be a domain of warfare.[37] In other words, they are not thinking only in terms of data held within and transmitted between computers and other electronic systems. Instead, they view information as an all-encompassing whole, of which only part is held in electronic media. So, for example, Russian planners will consider propaganda and hacking as part of the same domain, one that spans everything from cyber operations and spin, through to diplomacy and intimidation. Every act or instrument that carries with it an informational weight, and that can be used to compel or deter, is considered within the same discipline.[38] To their Western counterparts, this defies their basic notions as to how informational warfighting is structured,[39] but it is worth noting that the glossary of key information security terms produced the Military Academy of the General Staff includes no entry for the term 'cyber warfare' as a specific, distinct phenomenon.[40]

This holistic approach to information reflects not simply a tradition of using propaganda in aggressive statecraft dating back to the tsarist times yet honed under the Soviets, but also the Communist Party's determination to try and control information within its realm. The internet was very quickly identified as a potential threat, but it emerged at a time when the security apparatus was relatively weak and in no position to control it.[41] While attempts have been made, especially since 2013, to try and control online activity, instead the security structures had to accept that they operated in an information age and instead looked to means to exploit this.

Both the security agencies and the military began to explore how to extend information warfare, especially to attack enemy decision-making structures and command and control networks.[42] Through the 1990s and early 2000s, it became clear that the old Soviet means of information warfare, which had depended heavily on subversion and disinformation through ideological fellow travellers and front organisations, would no longer work. The online world became increasingly attractive. As with so many other aspects of military reform, it was the 2008 Georgian War that accelerated the process. Despite some successes in both manipulating Tbilisi to 'fire the first shot' (albeit in response to a carefully orchestrated series of provocations) and also in blocking its communications, the consensus was that Moscow could have done much better. As one Russian assessment put it, the war 'had shown our incapacity in defending our goals and interests in the global information space.'[43]

At first, the usual turf wars intruded. Originally, Russia's information operations capacity had been concentrated in FAPSI (the Federal Agency for Government Communications and Information) but in 2003 it was dissolved as an agency in a cannibalistic takeover that saw most of it transferred to the FSB, with some cryptographic and signals intelligence units going to the GRU and the primary secure communications system in the hands of the FSO (Federal Protection Service).[44] Even so, the FSB originally seems to have largely considered information operations from a defensive standpoint.

Especially after Georgia, the potential offensive opportunities of modern information operations came into sharp relief and, in line with the usual duplicative and competitive habits of Russian security services, the military moved aggressively to develop its own capabilities. The FSB spiritedly tried to maintain a near-monopoly, and a 2013 presidential decree tasked it with the primary role in detecting, preventing and mitigating cyberattacks against Russia, but the military's demand to develop its own 'Information Troops'[45] to prosecute 'information operations, which may encompass broad, socio-psychological manipulation' had taken fruit by the time of the seizure of Crimea.[46] As a result, the war in Ukraine has featured an interconnected information campaign involving everything from targeted propaganda, through direct terrorism, to varied cyberattacks.[47] However, this is essentially active measures in the virtual realm, or Messner's subversion war taken to the field. Far from new ways of war, in many ways both hybrid and political war can thus be seen as revivals of Soviet-era methods, adapted to the modern context.

Notes

1 Ken Booth, *Strategy and Ethnocentrism* (Holmes & Meier Publishers Inc., 1979), p. 144.
2 *Voenno-promyshlennyi kur'er*, 27 February 2013.
3 A. J. C. Selhorst, 'Russia's perception warfare,' *Militaire Spectator*, 185, 4 (2016), p. 148; CNN, 12 April 2018.
4 Chris Coons, 'Are we at war with Russia?' Brookings Institution, 7 April 2017 www.brookings.edu/blog/order-from-chaos/2017/04/07/are-we-at-war-with-russia/.

The view from the Kremlin   37

5 Asymmetric Warfare Group, *Russian New Generation Warfare Handbook* (US Army, 2016).

6 Mark Galeotti, 'The "Gerasimov Doctrine" and Russian non-linear war,' In Moscow's Shadows, 7 June 2014 https://inmoscowsshadows.wordpress. com/2014/07/06/the-gerasimov-doctrine-and-russian-non-linear-war/.

7 Mark Galeotti, 'The mythical "Gerasimov Doctrine" and the language of threat,' *Critical Studies on Security*, 6, 1 (2018); and 'I'm sorry for creating the "Gerasimov Doctrine",' *Foreign Policy*, 5 March 2018.

8 See also Roger McDermott, 'Does Russia have a Gerasimov Doctrine?' *Parameters*, 46, 1 (2016).

9 See, for example, Aleksei Kuz'movich, 'Evolutsiya vsglyadov na teoriyu sovremennoi voiny,' *Armiya i obshchestvo*, 33, 1 (2013).

10 Andrew Monaghan, *Russian State Mobilization: Moving the Country on to a War Footing* (Chatham House, 2016), p. 3.

11 Conversation, Moscow, April 2014.

12 Makmut Gareev, 'Voina i voennaya nauka na sovremennom.' *Voyenno-promyshlenniy kur'er*, 3 April 2013.

13 V. P. Gulin, 'O novoi kontseptsii voiny,' *Voennaya mysl'*, 6, 3 (1997).

14 Vladimir Kvachkov, *Spetsnaz Rossii* (Voennaya literatura, 2004), p. 127.

15 Sergei Chekinov and Sergei Bogdanov, 'Evolutsiya sushchnosti i soderzhaniya ponyatiya "voina" v XXI stoletii,' *Voennaya mysl'*, 26, 1 (2017), p. 78.

16 S. A. Tyshkevich (ed.), *Marksism-Leninism o voine i armii* (Voenizdat, 1974), p. 387.

17 *Vremya Novostei*, 5 October 2002, quoted in Roger McDermott, *Russian Perspective on Network-centric Warfare: the Key Aim of Serdyukov's Reform* (FMSO, 2010).

18 Conversation, Moscow, April 2016.

19 For an excellent analysis of this, see Roger McDermott, *Russian Perspective on Network-centric Warfare: the Key Aim of Serdyukov's Reform* (FMSO, 2010).

20 A. E. Savinkin and I. V. Domnin (eds), *Groznoe oruzhie: Malaya voina, partizanstvo i drugie vidy asimmetrichnogo voevaniya v svete naslediya russkikh voennykh myslitelei* (Russkii put', 2007).

21 Leon Trotsky, *What Next?* (1932) www.marxists.org/archive/trotsky/germany/1932-ger/.

22 Notably including I. V. Vuich, *Malaya voina* (E. Pratsa: 1850), I. P. Liprandi, *Nekotorye zamechaniya po povodu dvukh vyshedshikh pod zaglabiem 'malaya voina'* (MVD, 1851) and F. K. Gershel'man *Partizanskaya voina* (Departamenta Udelov, 1885).

23 M. A. Drobov, *Malaya voina: partizanstvo i diversii* (Voenizdat, 1931).

24 Merle Maigre, 'Nothing new in hybrid warfare: the Estonian experience and recommendations for NATO,' *German Marshall Fund of the United States Policy Brief*, February 2015.

25 I explore this in more detail in my 'Hybrid, ambiguous, and non-linear? How new is Russia's "new way of war"?' *Small Wars & Insurgencies*, 27, 2 (2016), pp. 282–301.

26 Georgii Isserson, *Evolutsiya operativnogo iskusstva* (1936), quote from *The Evolution of Operational Art* (Army University Press, 2013), translation by Bruce Menning, p. 98.
27 See Ofer Fridman, *Russian 'Hybrid' Warfare* (Hurst, 2018), pp. 49–74.
28 Evgenii Messner, 'Gore i pobezhdennym i pobeditelyam,' *Segodnya* 71 (1931), quoted in Ofer Fridman, *Russian 'Hybrid' Warfare* (Hurst, 2018), p. 57.
29 Evgenii Messner, *Myatezh: imya tret'yey vsemirnoy* (Golovin Institute, 1960), p. 43.
30 Evgenii Messner, *Vsemirnaya myatezhevoina* (Golovin Institute, 1971), p. 78, quoted in Ofer Fridman, *Russian 'Hybrid' Warfare* (Hurst, 2018), p. 67.
31 Personal correspondence, 1990.
32 Between 1921 and 1939, the euphemistic International Liaison Department (OMS) of the Moscow-based Communist International, Comintern, was a clandestine service engaged in running agents, subversion and, if need be, sabotage. Even before the Comintern was abolished in 1943, the OMS had been disbanded, but the international Communist movement continued to be used as a front and support base for the Soviet intelligence services.
33 See, for example, Maria Snegovaya, *Putin's Information Warfare in Ukraine*, ISW Russia Report No. 1 (2015); and Timothy Thomas, 'Russia's reflexive control theory and the military,' *Journal of Slavic Military Studies*, 17, 2 (2004).
34 See Victor Madeira, *Britannia and the Bear: The Anglo-Russian Intelligence Wars, 1917–1929* (Boydell, 2014); Ion Pacepa, *Disinformation* (WND, 2013); Steve Abrams, 'Beyond propaganda: Soviet active measures in Putin's Russia,' *Connections*, 15, 1 (2016).
35 Sergei Chekinov and Sergei Bogdanov, 'Vliyanie nepriamykh deistvii na kharakter sovremennoi voiny,' *Voennaya mysl'*, 20, 6 (2011), p. 7.
36 I am especially indebted to Keir Giles for useful input into this section.
37 Georgii Pocheptsov, *Informatsionnye voiny* (Refl-buk, 2001).
38 There is a rich body of Russian strategic thought on this. See, for example, Sergei Modestov, 'Strategicheskoe sderzhivanie na teatre informatsionnogo protivoborstva,' *Vestnik Akademii Voennykh Nauk*, 26, 1 (2009).
39 For good primer, see Ulrik Franke, *War by Non-military Means* (FOI, 2015).
40 *Slovar' terminov i opredeleniy v oblasti informatsionnoy bezopasnosti, 2nd edition,* (Voeninform, 2008).
41 Andrei Soldatov and Irina Borogan, *The Red Web* (PublicAffairs, 2017).
42 See V. M. Lisovoi, 'O zakonakh razvitiya vooruzhennoy bor'by i nekotorykh tendentsiyakh v oblasti oborony,' *Voennaya mysl'*, 3, 5 (1993).
43 *Voenno-promyshlennyi kur'er*, 15 October 2008.
44 Gordon Bennett, 'FPS and FAPSI – RIP,' *Conflict Studies Research Centre Occasional Brief*, 96 (2003).
45 Keir Giles, 'Information troops: a Russian cyber command?,' *Third International Conference on Cyber Conflict* (NATO Cooperative Cyber Defence Centre of Excellence, 2011).

46 Stephen Blank, 'Signs of new Russian thinking about the military and war,' *Eurasia Daily Monitor*, 12 February 2014; Volodymyr Lysenko and Catherine Brooks, 'Russian information troops, disinformation, and democracy,' *First Monday*, 23, 5 (2018).

47 Kenneth Geers (ed.), *Cyber War in Perspective: Russian Aggression against Ukraine* (NATO Cooperative Cyber Defence Centre of Excellence, 2015).

Part II
Wars hybrid and political

4   The Russian way of (real) war

> When I joined the army, back in 1987, I was trained in combined arms
> operations: tanks, motor rifle, artillery, frontal aviation. OK, now
> there are drones and other new toys, but at base, it's the same. That's a
> soldier's job, still.
>
> (Russian officer, 2014)[1]

In the current furore of discussions specifically about hybrid war, relatively few Western analysts – though, of course, there are honourable
exceptions[2] as well as a whole body of conventional military studies –
consider how the Russians themselves seem to expect wars to unfold.
The Russian military, after all, spends a great deal more time and money
preparing for conventional operations. As Michael Kofman has noted,
for example: 'Ukraine was decided by large-caliber artillery [multiple
launch rocket systems] and tanks; not innovative hybrid approaches.'[3]
A survey of the current state of Russian military thinking by the ubiquitous Chekinov and Bogdanov from 2011, in the heavyweight journal
Voennaya mysl' is still the closest thing to a blueprint for how Moscow
sees a modern, full-scale conflict developing. They wrote:

> A new-generation war will be dominated by information and psy-
> chological warfare that will seek to achieve superiority in troops
> and weapons control and depress the opponent's armed forces per-
> sonnel and population morally and psychologically. In the ongoing
> revolution in information technologies, information and psycho-
> logical warfare will largely lay the groundwork for victory.[4]

Thus, there would be a pre-conflict stage dominated by what could be
described as hybrid operations, in which

the aggressor [implicitly the West] will make an effort to involve all public institutions in the country it intends to attack, primarily the mass media and religious organisations, cultural institutions, non-governmental organisations, public movements financed from abroad, and scholars engaged in research on foreign grants.

Indeed,

[m]onths before the start of a new-generation war, large-scale measures in all types of warfare – information, moral, psychological, ideological, diplomatic, economic, and so on – may be designed and followed under a joint plan to create a favourable military, political, and economic setting for the operations of the allies' armed forces.

This is certainly about the kind of operations envisaged in Western projections of Russian hybrid war. However, once the information operations, cyberattacks,[5] misdirections and even, for real exotic value, 'nonlethal new-generation genetically engineered biological weapons' have had their day, Chekinov and Bogdanov see the war moving into its kinetic phase, a 'shock and awe' offensive reminiscent of the US-led Desert Storm offensive that shattered Saddam Hussein's Iraq in 1991. It would start with devastating aerial attacks and move eventually into a decisive ground combat phase:

[I]n the closing period of the war, the attacker will roll over the remaining points of resistance and destroy surviving enemy units by special operations conducted by reconnaissance units to spot what enemy units have survived and transmit their co-ordinates to the attacker's missile and artillery units; fire barrages to annihilate the defender's resisting army units by effective advanced weapons; airdrop operations to surround points of resistance; and territory mopping-up operations by ground troops.

At the very time that Moscow is exploring the less-than-war options at its disposal, then – or at least how to combat them – it is also planning, training and equipping for high-tempo conventional warfare. This is best demonstrated by the scale and nature of its ambitious training and exercises regime, which is clearly oriented towards such engagements.[6] If Russia ever truly goes to war, it will do so with massive, intense bombardments, combined air, sea and land operations, and all the rest of the pyrotechnic panoply of modern warfare. This, not the semi-covert, spooks-and-trolls hybrid wars often imagined in the West, is what they train for, this is what they are spending their money on, and this is at the heart of Russian military thinking and writing.

Learning lessons

All military doctrines are an evolution of previous ones, and influenced by the technical, political, social and economic forces shaping the battlefield at every level. Today's Russian approach is broadly rooted in some distinctive characteristics of modern Russia and in past practice, but more specifically it is the product of a series of military-political debates and organisational developments that came to fruition following the 2008 Georgian War, as well as their take on Western thinking.[7] The 1979–1988 incursion into Afghanistan had forced Soviet military planners to come to grips with asymmetric war, but many of the lessons were deliberately shelved at the time, the result of a foolishly optimistic assumption that Moscow would never again be embroiled in such campaigns.[8] Nonetheless, the experience of that conflict (and the disastrous First Chechen War) did creep into subsequent debates in the 1990s, where they combined with a growing awareness of the sheer speed and destructiveness of modern conflict. Longer-ranged weapons, computerised guidance and launch systems, advanced ISR (intelligence, surveillance and reconnaissance) capacities, all these would mean that in full-scale war, the front line would be deep, perhaps even ubiquitous, and the potential devastation of this 'non-contact warfare,' terrifying.

To some, the answer was to put all the more emphasis on winning the war before the first shot was fired, or at least to get as close to that as possible. In Makhmut Gareev's thoughtful 1995 study *Esli zavtra voina* (*If War Comes Tomorrow?*), for example, he noted that political and information operations could be used to spread 'mass psychosis, despair and feelings of doom and undermine trust in the government and armed forces; and, in general, lead to the destabilisation of the situation in those countries' ready for direct intervention.[9] One might even say he had discovered his inner Messner.

Nonetheless, through the 1990s, the conflict in Chechnya and the challenge coping in severely constrained budgetary circumstances continued to consume much of whatever scope there was for doctrinal innovation. A Russian officer serving in the General Staff at the time recalled that 'the intellectual case for change was always accepted, then "temporarily" shelved until the day's crisis was resolved. But, there was always another crisis.'[10] The 2000 National Security Concept document and new Military Doctrine and a 2003 White Paper on defence did place a far greater emphasis than in the past on joint military–security agency cooperation, internal wars and irregular conflicts, but primarily in the context of dealing with purely domestic insurgency. Many within the Russian security establishment genuinely understood that the nature of war was changing. However, all such institutions tend towards conservatism, and a combination of self-interested resistance within the high command and a lack of a clear steer from the Kremlin ensured that practice did not move as quickly as the theoretical discussions.

Real progress would only follow as a result of the Georgian War. Russian forces operated alongside local militias and auxiliaries, in a politically choreographed operation designed to provide a degree of deniability and legitimacy by provoking the Georgians into the first overt act of aggression.[11] Even beforehand, Moscow had been exploring such ambiguous and arm's-length options, but the practical experience of the war proved a crucial agent for change. The Russians won, but that was hardly in doubt given the massive disproportion between the two sides and Moscow's relatively limited objectives, 'liberating' the already-rebellious regions of Abkhazia and South Ossetia. However, sufficient problems emerged to allow Defence Minister Anatolii Serdyukov and, above all, his Chief of the General Staff Nikolai Makarov finally to push through sweeping reforms. Organisationally, the main change was a transition to a smaller, more flexible brigade structure – first mooted, after all, back in Soviet times[12] – but this also unblocked the way to deeper doctrinal debates within the military, not least adapting to the notion of network-centric warfare.

Big war

Serdyukov, whose necessary but brutal reform programme won him the loathing of most of the officer corps, would not survive long politically; a scandal saw him sacked in 2012, with Makarov following in his wake. However, their successors continued the process, hence the irony of Gerasimov getting the credit for what, if it should be considered any Chief of the General Staff's brainchild, was closer to Makarov's. Even so, this was still very much a discussion about conventional military conflict, not deniable, political, hybrid war.

Bērziņš is absolutely right when he says:

> The Russian view of modern warfare is based on the idea that the main battlespace is the mind and, as a result, new-generation wars are to be dominated by information and psychological warfare, in order to achieve superiority in troops and weapons control, morally

and psychologically depressing the enemy's armed forces personnel and civil population.[13]

However, it is important to note that this is simply about a greater role for informational and political operations in support of the essentially kinetic. According to Colonel General Andrei Kartapolov, formerly head of General Staff's Main Operations Directorate – its primary planning division and, in many ways, the brain of the armed forces – and then head of its Main Political-Military Affairs Directorate, whereas once wars were 80% fighting and 20% propaganda, now they are 80–90% propaganda and 10–20% fighting.[14] But they still depend on armed force to finish things. So the army still expects to soldier, but will gladly take advantage of the opportunities to demoralise and distract the enemy – just as it expects the foe to be trying to do the same.

Looking at Russia's recent set-piece exercises can be instructive. While there is inevitably always an element of theatre and bluster in such extravaganzas, as will be discussed, these are too expensive and important to be wholly staged as propaganda and not primarily be designed to train and test soldiers for the wars they are expected to fight.[15] The 2017 *Zapad* ('West') exercise, was officially kept to fewer than 10,000 soldiers (to preclude the West demanding to send observers under the terms of the Organization for Security and Co-operation in Europe's (OSCE) 2011 Vienna Document), but probably included closer to 65,000–70,000 thanks to both creative accounting and packaging together several smaller exercises into the same overall plan.[16] Interestingly, it started with wargaming a defence against a hybrid attack, enemy special forces invading in support of foreign-inspired terrorists, to be met with infantry, tanks, artillery and air strikes. The exercise also included the paramilitary internal security troops of the National Guard, again an indicator that there is a real concern about insurgency at home. Next year, the Russian Far East saw the much larger *Vostok* ('East') exercises, which, outside the OSCE's purview, officially involved some 300,000 troops (and almost 5,000 Chinese and Mongolians), although in practice the real figure was likely at most half that. Even so, that time the wargames essentially focused on a conventional peer-to-peer clash, with neither the enemy ('blue') nor the home ('red') side using much in the way of hybrid tactics, beyond a few special forces raids. Moscow seems to see a *gibridnaya voina* threat from the west, but not the east.

In short, if one looks at Russian military writings and triangulates them with their doctrine and their exercises, this is not a force preparing in the main for 'non-linear,' small-scale, semi-covert operations. What is sometimes now called 'new generation warfare' – another problematic formulation given that there is always a newer generation, but at least it is one the Russians themselves use – envisages their use in a limited, initial stage of a conflict. The Russians will use special forces, jamming, cyber operations, long-range strikes and other means to spread chaos, of course. More broadly, though, there is a clear belief that they are more likely to be the target rather than the master of *gibridnaya voina*. In any case, its answer to Western non-linear operations and active measures is traditionally Russian and reassuringly military: massive firepower. If we want to find a locus and a constituency for subtle political subversion as an alternative to all-out war, we need to move from the General Staff's building west of the Kremlin to Old Square to the east, and the sprawling offices of the Presidential Administration.

Notes

1 Conversation, 2014.
2 Notably, although not exclusively, Pavel Baev, Dmitry Gorenburg, Michael Kofman, Roger McDermott and Andrew Monaghan.
3 Michael Kofman, 'Russian hybrid warfare and other dark arts,' War on the Rocks, 11 March 2016 http://warontherocks.com/2016/03/russian-hybrid-warfare-and-other-dark-arts/.
4 This and the quotes that follow are from Sergei Chekinov and Sergei Bogdanov, 'Vliyanie nepriamykh deistvii na kharakter sovremennoi voiny,' *Voennaya mysl'*, 20, 6 (2011).
5 Their use, especially in this pre-war phase, is also explored in Pavel Antonovich, 'O sushchnosti i soderzhanii kibervoiny,' *Voennaya mysl'*, 20, 7 (2011). In addition, see Timothy Thomas, 'Russia's information warfare strategy: can the nation cope in future conflicts?' *Journal of Slavic Military Studies*, 27, 1 (2014).
6 Johan Norberg, *Training to Fight – Russia's Major Military Exercises 2011–2014* (FOI, 2015).
7 Marcel De Haas, 'Russia's military doctrine development 2000–2010,' in Stephen Blank (ed.), *Russia's Military Politics and Russia's 2010 Defense Doctrine* (Strategic Studies Institute, 2011), pp. 1–62.
8 Mark Galeotti, *Afghanistan: the Soviet Union's Last War* (Frank Cass, 1995), chapter 11.
9 Makhmut Gareev, *Esli zavtra voina* (Vladar, 1995); quote from English translation, *If War Comes Tomorrow? The Contours of Future Armed Conflict* (Routledge, 1998), pp. 51–52.
10 Conversation, Moscow, January 2014.
11 According to the European Union's *Independent International Fact-Finding Mission on the Conflict in Georgia* (2009), the so-called 'Tagliavini Report.'

12 See Robert Hall, *Soviet Military Art in a Time of Change* (Palgrave Macmillan, 1990).

13 Jānis Bērziņš, *Russia's New Generation Warfare in Ukraine: Implications for Latvian Defence Policy*, Policy Paper 2, Centre for Security and Strategic Research, National Defence Academy of Latvia, 6 April 2014, p. 5.

14 Andrei Kartapolov, 'Uroki voennykh konfliktov, perspektivy razvitiya sredstv i sposobov ikh vedeniya. Pryamie i nepryamie deistviya v sovremennykh mezhdunarodnykh konfliktakh,' *Vestnik Akademii Voennykh Nauk*, 51, 2 (2015), p. 33.

15 Johan Norberg, *Training to Fight – Russia's Major Military Exercises 2011–2014* (FOI, 2015).

16 Igor Sutyagin, 'Zapad-2017: why do the numbers matter?' *RUSI Commentary*, 12 September 2017.

5 Political war in theory

The Russian military talk a great deal about what they do, what they want to be able to do and how they expect to do it. In part, this is necessary when trying to create a unified body of military thought across an institution with over a million personnel and some 40 military schools and academies. There is also a long tradition of sometimes surprisingly candid debate in specialist publications such as *Voennaya mysl'* (*Military Thought*) and *Voennyi vestnik* (*Military Herald*). As a result, we have a pretty good sense of the tides and trends in these discussions, even while all kinds of detail will remain classified or take time to percolate into view.

From the Arbat to Old Square

This helps explain why outside perceptions of Russian strategy have been shaped disproportionately by the military's debates. But if the strategists and planners of the so-called 'Arbat Military District' (because of the General Staff's historic location on Znamenka Street in the Arbat neighbourhood) have made much of the running in exploring how 'hybrid' non-military means can help shape the battlefield, that is not the same as Russian national security thinking. As will be discussed in more detail in the next chapter, this is much more the purview of the Presidential Administration (*Administratsiya prezidenta*, AP) on Staraya (Old) Square and the Security Council (*Sovet bezopasnosti*, SB) on Ipatevskii Alley, technically part of the AP but in many ways functionally distinct.

It is crucial to stress the primacy of the political leadership and the apparatus through which it governs. Russia, like the Soviet Union, has a relatively powerful, well-resourced and self-confident military. The defence minister's position can be a very significant one, although this inevitably depends on the individual. The current incumbent, Sergei

Shoigu, is a serious player. He has an enviable track record of institutional success, not least in the creation of the Ministry of Emergency Situations in the 1990s, turning a collection of near-dysfunctional services into a working and – by Russian standards – relatively honest and effective agency. He has public recognition, a good personal relationship with Putin and the almost unheard-of ability to rise through this system without seeming to make enemies. For all that, though, he is clearly a subordinate, one able to argue positions and advocate policy, but ultimately subject to the presidential will. In this, he fits into a strong tradition of the control of the military; always fearful of 'Bonapartism' and the potential intrusion of the generals into government, the Communist Party kept a firm grip on them, and even Boris Yeltsin, in his own way, maintained his authority over the generals. Putin has been no less assiduous in making sure that he is unquestionably the man in charge, not least through his choices of civilian defence ministers: fellow KGB veteran and close ally Sergei Ivanov (2001–2007), tax official and dependent client Anatolii Serdyukov (2007–2012) and then Shoigu.

While the ministry and the General Staff play an important role in formulating military plans, policy reflects wider political calculations. Sometimes, these are specific and public, such as the memorable moment in 2011 when Putin overruled Serdyukov's decision – at the urging of his own generals – not to order more tanks. The military felt their existing T-72s, suitably upgraded, were enough, and had other spending priorities, but Putin was courting the defence industrial vote, so there needed to be orders. More generally, though, the national security documents from which military doctrine flows are produced by the Security Council, and while the generals undoubtedly contribute to their discussions, theirs is not the deciding voice.

The national security apparatus will be explored further, but the key point is that its deliberations are much less overtly public than those of the military. Sometimes internal debates spill out into rival op-ed pieces in newspapers or the like, but the participants are generally officials rather than public figures and the culture is secretive. They do, however, share a belief that Russia is being constrained, even threatened, by a West too powerful directly to challenge, and have thus been looking for new instruments of contestation. Ivanov went from the defence ministry to then become the powerful presidential chief of staff and head of the AP 2011–2016; meanwhile, since 2008 the SB has been chaired by fellow hawk and KGB veteran Nikolai Patrushev. Having himself learnt his trade as a spy, built his career on corruption and behind-the-scenes politicking, and forged a presidency through propaganda and hype, Putin likewise seems to have seen the scope for 'political war' rooted in Soviet practices. The two variations of *gibridnaya voina* were ready to be born.

Political war

> Political warfare is the logical application of Clausewitz's doctrine in time of peace. In broadest definition, political warfare is the employment of all the means at a nation's command, short of war, to achieve its national objectives. Such operations are both overt and covert. They range from such overt actions as political alliances, economic measures (as ERP – the Marshall Plan), and 'white' propaganda to such covert operations as clandestine support of 'friendly' foreign elements, 'black' psychological warfare and even encouragement of underground resistance in hostile states.
>
> (George Kennan, 1948)[1]

The practice goes back to prehistory,[2] but the real emergence of political war as a concept in the West was rooted in the Allied psychological warfare campaigns of the Second World War, revived and reinterpreted by Kennan as the Cold War loomed. (In other words, again this is a notion with an American pedigree.) Kennan was in particular 'critiquing American policymakers' continuing predilection for thinking in terms of a war-peace binary' – something that arguably survives to the present day[3] – and instead look to consider a basis for sustained, coordinated and purposeful attempts to undermine the Soviet system, which would not degenerate into war.[4]

Hoffman has made it clear that he is unhappy with the formulation 'political war,' considering it 'imprecise – if not redundant' because all wars are political and the term 'warfare' should only mean specifically the physical conduct of war or the fighting and violent aspects of war.[5] The former point is entirely true, but the second bears some scrutiny. First of all, one could suggest that, in general usage, the battle for the purity of the concept of 'warfare' has already been lost. At a time when disinformation, hacking and leaking data are widely described as 'hybrid war' when not a shot has been fired, to say nothing of the use of such hyperbolic phrases as 'the war on drugs,' then the requirement that one can only use the term to the sound of the guns may no longer truly apply. One could call it 'political conflict' but that simply opens up the reasonable counter-argument that almost all politics are conflictual to some degree. Besides, much political warfare is hardly bloodless: assassinations, stirring up violent mobs, working through thugs and terrorists, and even deploying small-scale military forces are all clearly part of the toolbox. Coercion, if not openly declared war, is central to political warfare and what truly distinguishes it from the more silken suasions of soft power. Given that Russian practice most closely seems to follow Kennan's own formulation, it seems most appropriate to use it – even though *politicheskaya voina* is not a term one will often find in their writings – rather than generating some neologism to re-label, if not reinvent, the wheel. The Putin regime is embarked on a campaign against the West that it considers to be equivalent to a war – and yet which it is determined to keep within the realms of the political, to keep it 'short of war.' This is, after all, something that was likewise embraced by Kennan's contemporaries and his intellectual heirs. In 1952, at a gathering of government luminaries convened at Princeton to consider how the USA could use political warfare against the USSR, Lewis Galantiere, Head of Propaganda Policy at Radio Free Europe, characterised it as

> [t]he sum of the activities in which a government engages for the attainment of its objectives without unleashing armed warfare. But it is a description which applies to none of those activities when each of them is carried on independently of the others. In that case they become 'mere' diplomacy, intelligence, propaganda, economic negotiation, armament production, and so on. The essence of political warfare is that it is planned and the means employed to carry it on are coordinated.[6]

It may be hard to draw precise boundaries between real war and political war, and between soft power and hard-nosed diplomacy (although Messner tried with his four states formulation), but nonetheless in their own hazy and often subjective way, these lines exist.[7] Furthermore, as Galantiere noted, the key issue is that while political war involves a wide range of familiar and even banal instruments, what makes it a meaningful concept is when they are brought together in coordinated, purposeful form.

Soviet political war

> My dear [American] friends, I think you are in big trouble. Whether you believe it or not, YOU ARE AT WAR … An integral part of this ideological war is IDEOLOGICAL SUBVERSION.
> (Soviet defector Yuri Bezmenov, 1984)[8]

Today's Russia is certainly no Soviet Union 2.0, but its strategic culture nonetheless cannot help but be influenced by its forebears. The Bolsheviks were especially keen students of Clausewitz. Lenin himself directly quoted him, and had a heavily annotated notebook of readings and comments on his work.[9] From the very first – again, often reflecting their sense of being arrayed against more objectively powerful enemies – they adopted a flexible approach to geopolitics that sought to mobilise any advantages and sidestep vulnerabilities, regardless of the formal boundaries between war and peace, legal and illicit.[10] The Communist International – Comintern – may have been founded in the name of an ideal, but this Moscow-based assembly of Communist parties became, like its successor Cominform, essentially a covert arm of Soviet state power and interests, a way of using ideology to acquire capabilities to subvert and coerce abroad. Fellow travellers were ruthlessly cultivated and even more ruthlessly exploited, sometimes to become intelligence assets, but otherwise to spread propaganda in Moscow's interests. In the inter-war period, the Soviets involved themselves in the Spanish Civil War, but later, a wide range of anti-colonial movements and other insurgent and terrorist groups would be seduced, supported and subverted as proxy agents in the Cold War.

While the Soviet leadership was perfectly willing to use open military force when it felt that was indicated, *aktivnye meropriyatiya* or 'active measures' – a term used from the 1950s to cover the gamut of political influence and subversion operations – were truly central to their wider strategy. Of course, this is not to say that such methods were unique to the Soviets; as noted above, the United States, and the West as a whole, was also engaged in their own political and psychological campaigns, which often seemed little different in scale and cynical pragmatism from those of the Soviets. A feature especially of the early Cold War era, the US campaign would also be reinvigorated by Ronald Reagan's National Security Decision Directive Number 32 (NSDD-32) of 1982, which committed the USA 'to contain and reverse the expansion of Soviet control and military presence throughout the world' and 'to encourage long-term liberalizing and nationalist tendencies within the Soviet Union and allied countries.'[11] This was nothing less than a declaration of political war to the knife.[12] However, what was different was the degree and consistency to which the political and the military were integrated in Soviet planning and practice and, indeed, the amount of theoretical attention this was given.

Yuri Bezmenov, a Soviet journalist and propagandist who defected to the West in 1970, affirmed that the main emphasis of the KGB is not in the area of intelligence at all ... Only about 15% of time, money and manpower is spent on espionage and such. The other 85% is a slow process which we call either ideological subversion or active measures.[13]

One can treat the numbers with distinct caution, but nonetheless accept that the KGB certainly considered its mission as being to change the world at least as much as to spy on it – in contrast with most intelligence services, which consider their primary mission being to provide policy-makers with the 'best truth' they can. The KGB manufactured 'evidence' supporting claims that AIDS was a US biological warfare agent under experimentation.[14] It supported useful political movements – many of which had no idea the Soviets were trying to use them as political warfighting instruments – from the Campaign for Nuclear Disarmament to the Afro-Asian People's Solidarity Organisation.[15] State-controlled media spun and spread disinformation, and even economic institutions were considered an arm of the wider geopolitical campaigns. The Paris-based but Soviet-controlled Banque Commerciale pour l'Europe du Nord, for example, funded local Communist parties and even engaged in attempts to interfere in global markets.[16] In short, active measures were integral to Soviet thought and practice about its external relations and its struggle with the capitalist West (and, in due course, a revisionist China).

Russian political war

Soviet active measures were flexible and often opportunistic, but overall strategic control was exercised through the Communist Party Central Committee's international and information departments, before cascading down through the foreign ministry, the state media and the KGB, notably Service A of its foreign intelligence arm, the First Chief Directorate. It is perhaps glib but worth noting that the offices once held by the Central Committee today house the Presidential Administration. Likewise, the KGB's First Chief Directorate was essentially hived off to become the present SVR, even keeping the same headquarters at Yasenevo, in Moscow's southern suburbs. Continuity of administrative geography does not predetermine continuity of policy, but it certainly does happen to reflect the extent to which Putin's Russia has built on Soviet practices, albeit freed from the admittedly weak shackles of ideology and empowered by the modern communications revolution.

At the 2018 Valdai Club, a gathering of Russian and foreign experts that culminates in a set-piece appearance by Putin himself, one of the doyens of the Moscow foreign policy community chose to 'out' this strategy in a thoughtfully damning speech. Andrei Kortunov – liberal scholar, one-time diplomat, think-tanker and policy adviser – warned that the 'victory of the paradigm of war over the paradigm of politics, over the paradigm of diplomacy' in Russia, had been marked by 'the expansion of a military mindset to non-military aspects of world politics.' He went on:

> They say that all means are fair in love and war, including disinformation, deception, and provocation. But this should not be the case in politics, where reputation, predictability and reliability are very important. ... It seems that we all – in East and West – are beginning to live according to the laws of wartime, when all means are good, and reputation becomes an unaffordable luxury or, at least, an easily spent resource. And as a result, for example, a very important red line between politics and a special operation is practically erased.[17]

The essence of political war is precisely often that it is undeclared and unacknowledged, and it took an uncomfortable insider to highlight this new policy of 'diplomacy with a military mindset' where politics, spycraft and propaganda are virtually indistinguishable. The view of today's Russian national security establishment is thus epitomised by the words of Alexander Vladimirov, a man spanning both the worlds of the generals and the national security policy team as a retired major general and chair of the military experts' panel at the influential think-tank, the Russian International Affairs Council. In 2007, just at the time when a new note of geopolitical confrontation was beginning to creep into official Kremlin statements, he wrote that 'modern wars are waged on the level of consciousness and ideas' and that 'modern humanity exists in a state of permanent war ... eternally oscillating between phases of actual armed struggle and constant preparation for it.'[18] This neatly summarises the mindset that appears dominant within the Kremlin and its apparatus, and the thinking behind political war.

It also helps explain the choice of essentially political tactics. In 2014, an otherwise sober-minded think-tanker with good links to the Presidential Administration, in the middle of a conversation with me about how Moscow could assert its claims to great-power status, disconcertingly quoted Igor Panarin, a KGB veteran turned professor and pundit known for his often extreme nationalist views.[19] In a book on information warfare, Panarin wrote that 'political activity is an

informational struggle over the minds of the elites and social groups.'[20]
'That,' my interlocutor said, 'that's how we'll do it.'

Notes

1 George Kennan's memo of 4 May 1948, 'The inauguration of organized political warfare,' State Department Office of the History online collection https://history.state.gov/historicaldocuments/frus1945-50Intel/d269.
2 Roy Godson and Richard Schultz, 'Soviet active measures: distinctions and definitions,' *Defence Analysis*, 1, 2 (1985), p. 101.
3 As Scott Harr asserts, US military planning is still dominated by the 'long-held paradigm of U.S. approaches to warfare [which] necessitates that combat power be dedicated toward the destruction of the enemy.' Scott Harr, 'Expanding Tolstoy and shrinking Dostoyevsky,' *Military Review*, Sept.–Oct. 2017, p. 41.
4 Sonya Lynn Finley, 'Recommending political warfare – the role of Eisenhower's Presidential Committee on international information activities in the United States' approach to the Cold War,' unpublished PhD dissertation, Virginia Polytechnic Institute and State University, 2016, p. 78, fn 43.
5 Frank Hoffman, 'On not-so-new warfare: political warfare vs hybrid threats,' War on the Rocks, 28 July 2014 https://warontherocks.com/2014/07/on-not-so-new-warfare-political-warfare-vs-hybrid-threats/.
6 From an initial working paper distributed at the meeting; quoted in Sonya Lynn Finley, 'Recommending political warfare – the role of Eisenhower's Presidential Committee on international information activities in the United States' approach to the Cold War,' unpublished PhD dissertation, Virginia Polytechnic Institute and State University, 2016, p. 90.
7 This is a point Angelo Codevilla explores in 'Political warfare: means for achieving political ends,' in J. Michael Waller (ed.), *Strategic Influence: Public Diplomacy, Counterpropaganda, and Political Warfare* (Institute of World Politics Press, 2009), pp. 206–223.
8 In his pseudonymous book, Tomas D. Schuman, *Love Letter to America* (Almanac Panorama, 1984), p. 5.
9 Donald Davis and Walter Kohn, 'Lenin's "Notebook on Clausewitz,"' *Soviet Armed Forces Review Annual*, 1 (1977), pp. 188–229.
10 See Victor Madeira, *Britannia and the Bear: The Anglo-Russian Intelligence Wars, 1917–1929* (Boydell, 2014).
11 NSDD-32, 20 May 1982 https://fas.org/irp/offdocs/nsdd/nsdd-32.pdf.
12 For a good overview, see Seth Jones, *A Covert Action: Reagan, the CIA and a Cold War Struggle in Poland* (W. W. Norton, 2018).
13 In an interview now on YouTube www.youtube.com/watch?v=mqSV72VNnV0.
14 'Long before Facebook, the KGB spread fake news about AIDS,' NPR, 22 August 2018 www.npr.org/2018/08/22/640883503/long-before-facebook-the-kgb-spread-fake-news-about-aids.

15 Loch Johnson, *Strategic Intelligence* (Greenwood, 2007), p. 42.
16 CIA Directorate of Intelligence, 'Soviet-owned banks in the West,' (1969), CIA Historical Review Program release ER IR 69–28.
17 Andrei Kortunov's 18 October 2018 speech is on the Valdai website http://russiancouncil.ru/analytics-and-comments/analytics/politika-kak-prodolzhenie-voyny-inymi-sredstvami/.
18 Alexander Vladimirov, *Kontseptualnye osnovy natsionalnoi strategii Rossii: Voyennopoliticheskii aspekt* (Nauka, 2007), pp. 105, 130.
19 Conversation, Moscow, March 2014.
20 Igor Panarin, *Informatsionnaya voina i geopolitika* (Pokolenie, 2006), p. 165.

6   Political war in action

Political war? I suppose. I suppose we are at war, and it is certainly
political.

(Former Presidential Administration staffer,
asked about the term, 2018)[1]

The military rattles sabres in the Baltic and the Black Sea. Diplomats
castigate Western 'Russophobia' and cultivate populist sentiment. The
media sell Russia as a peaceable neighbour and a bastion of traditional
social values. Spies bug, snoop and compromise, as if still at the height
of the Cold War. Hackers and trolls mount a 24/7 onslaught on Western
systems and discourses. Moscow deploys all sorts of different approaches
and different narratives, each of which plays to different strengths and
brings to the fore different agencies.[2] To some, this multi-vectored
challenge represents an extraordinarily complex and disciplined campaign, geopolitics as three-dimensional chess.[3] And yet, it is clear that
many, even most, individual initiatives are largely unconnected, often
opportunistic, their moves shaped by local conditions, concerns and
considerations. They connect only sometimes, and frequently clumsily.
There appears to be no detailed masterplan, but rather a broad strategy
of weakening the European Union (EU) and NATO, distancing Europe
and the United States from each other, and generally creating a political
and cultural environment more conducive for Moscow and its interests.

There is clearly some effort to coordinate certain operations across
platforms. Often this happens after an initiative is taken by individual
agents and actors. For example, in the infamous 2016 'Lisa Case' (in
which a 13-year-old Russian-German girl was reported to have been
kidnapped and raped by Turkish or Arab men, a story later proven to
be groundless), initial social media accounts were then recycled in the
Russian media, and subsequently cited by Russia's foreign minister,

Sergei Lavrov.[4] The Kremlin was simply reacting to, and trying to exploit, something that started independently. It is also worth noting that this campaign in many ways backfired: the girl recanted, and the German political elite – not least Chancellor Angela Merkel – were clearly outraged by this interference.

Political war from below

Russia's is a broad-based campaign in which the majority of individual ventures spring from the initiative of individuals within and without the government apparatus, guided by their sense of the Kremlin's desires rather than any detailed masterplan. What emerges from all kinds of different sources, open and closed, is that Putin himself tends not to be an originator; he would much rather arbitrate between rival approaches, pick from a menu of options or give people enough rope to hang or lift themselves. As one former Presidential Administration staffer put it:

> [W]e would push plans and options up, and eventually get some kind of response back. But it was rare that we'd actually get tasked from the boss [Putin] out of nowhere. I say 'rare': I can't actually think of a time when that happened.[5]

Instead, the Kremlin has adopted an innovative and parsimonious approach that, in effect, mobilises the ambitions and imaginations of sundry adhocrats, actors and agencies. It sets broad objectives and aspirations: to assert Russia's claim to great-power status; to consolidate dominance over its self-proclaimed sphere of influence; to weaken and distract the West such that it cannot offer any meaningful counters to Russian actions; to undermine hostile governments; and to shatter inconvenient structures such as NATO and the EU. The detail is sometimes, maybe even often, left deliberately open. Thus individuals and agencies scramble to identify how they can use the instruments and opportunities at their disposal in ways they hope will further these ends and please the Kremlin.

   Sometimes, they show promise and the Kremlin will throw its weight behind an initiative, or simply signal its approval. Even this diffuse, initiative-driven system requires certain mechanisms to work, after all. In a perverse return to the days of Kremlinology, when Soviets and foreigners alike would seek meaning in who signed which documents first and who stood where to review the parade on Red Square, Putin's public pronouncements are carefully scrutinised for clues, along with key government-controlled sources such as the newspaper *Rossiiskaya Gazeta*, as well as those favourites of the moment deemed to speak with their master's voice. In propaganda, for example, *Vesti Nedeli*, the weekly news programme hosted by Dmitrii Kiselev, head of the Russia Today news conglomerate, has become an implicit source of guidance on the official line – at least for that week. His jazz-handed diatribes are taken as hints as to the Kremlin's mood and interests. Then there are more explicit forms of guidance. Presidential Press Secretary Dmitrii Peskov meets the editors of the main government media platforms in the Kremlin each Friday to outline the expected – required – lines and topics for the week ahead.[6] These are supplemented by written secret guidance memoranda known as *temniki*. The 'troll farms' pumping out disinformation get their daily and weekly targets and talking points. Telegrams from the foreign ministry guide the activities of Russia's embassies abroad.

At other times, self-started actors and initiatives will stumble and fall, and the Kremlin can deny any role, or distance itself from them. Outspoken 'Eurasianist' Russian nationalist Alexander Dugin has, for example, at times been elevated to a virtual ideological spokesman of the state, then excluded when convenient.[7] He is a key exponent of the notion of the cultural and linguistic *Russkii mir*, a 'Russian world' wherever Russians are to be found. This was used in 2014 to rationalise support for the manufactured rebellion in the Donbas, and as outreach to ethnic Russians in the Baltic States. However, since then, the language of the *Russkii mir* and Dugin's own position within Moscow's narratives have declined markedly.[8] Despite heated claims about his influence in US alt-right circles and Moscow alike, Dugin's neo-fascist rhetoric had, by late 2015 or early 2016, been deemed counter-productive, and so he was again put on the shelf.[9]

There are certainly some operations that require explicit approval from the Kremlin. In some cases it is when some initiative from below is chosen to receive greater attention, and in others because the move has been launched from above. For example, in 2016 Finland faced a coordinated campaign to block any attempt to join NATO. The tempo of hostile trolling and disinformation picked up strikingly, with the addition of dubious but eye-catching claims that Lenin had not had the right to grant Finland independence in 1917, such that it could still be considered Russian territory.[10] Putin himself broadly hinted at retaliation if Helsinki made such moves, including new troop deployments on the Russo-Finnish border.[11] As if to illustrate the point, later in the year, literally hours after Helsinki signed a limited defence cooperation pact with the US, Russian warplanes made incursions into Finnish airspace.[12] This was clearly not random, but a deliberate, multi-vector campaign of intimidation.

It is hard to determine any hard and fast rule, but it appears to be that anything requiring cross-agency coordination will need at least some kind of approval from above. Whether it makes it all the way to Putin's desk depends on the scale of the operation and potential risk. According to a Bulgarian intelligence officer, for example, Russian national businessman Konstantin Malofeev, very active on both economic acquisitions and political networking in the Balkans since 2014,[13] originated the idea for an attempted coup in Montenegro in 2016 to forestall its joining NATO. Realising that this ultimately was too big for him to launch on his own initiative, he shopped the idea around Moscow. Security Council Chief Nikolai Patrushev liked the idea, sold it to Putin and took it over.[14] Such activities, which will clearly have some major political or economic fallout, such as the American Democratic National Committee leaks (though not necessarily the cyber espionage operations that preceded them), and the 2006 Litvinenko and 2018 Skripal cases, would certainly require approval to go ahead, whether from Putin for truly important ones, or otherwise from some other figure in his circle with that authority.[15]

The Presidential Administration: the hidden controller

On a strategic level, Putin sets the tone. On a tactical level, a series of ways exists of exerting control, typically within specific sectors. But what of the all-important operational level that connects the two, which provides whatever command and control exists within this diffuse campaign? Peskov – despite his bizarre role in the so-called 'Steele Dossier' as the reputed coordinator of a grand Kremlin political operation to suborn and elect Donald Trump[16] – lacks the time, experience or authority to work outside the realm of the media. None of the ministries has the power to tell the others what to do. The foreign ministry, which would appear to be the closest fit, has actually seen its power eroding steadily.[17] Even diplomatic service insiders glumly acknowledge that 'we are often called on to support other ministries, not the other way round.'[18]

The intelligence agencies exist largely in a state of competition with one another. The Security Council (SB), notionally part of the Presidential Administration, but in effect an autonomous agency, is tasked with coordinating all security-related issues – which the active measures campaign could be considered – and it is essentially a forum for the promulgation of instructions from above and the resolution of jurisdictional disputes. Its secretary, Nikolai Patrushev, is an FSB veteran close to Putin and a trusted enforcer and spook-watcher. As such, one could regard it as the possible command-and-control nexus. However, its secretariat is far too small for such a role. Its total strength is unclear, but it had 200 staff on Putin's accession to power in 2000, and, while this is likely to have grown to an extent, it has not expanded beyond its existing offices on Ipatevskii Alley. As well as supporting the regular meetings of the SB, the secretariat is also charged with providing it with analytic support, drafting documents including periodic revision of the National Security Strategy, and monitoring the implementation of presidential instructions. One government insider threw up his hands at the suggestion that the Security Council played a major role in the formulation of active measures strategy: 'Seriously, these guys [already] have more than enough on.'[19]

Furthermore, Patrushev is himself a player, not a referee. In particular, he increasingly appears to be emerging as the Kremlin's point man on the Balkans, especially since 2016, as the Russians begin to take the region more seriously.[20] After the failed Montenegro coup, it was Patrushev who hurriedly travelled to Belgrade to assuage local anger at an operation being launched from Serbian soil and also to arrange the quiet return to Moscow of three Russian intelligence officers to avoid a public scandal.[21]

In so far as there is a command-and-control centre, it appears to be the Presidential Administration. This is a much larger organisation than the SB, with almost 2,000 staffers, as well as the capacity to task various government and even outside bodies with analytic and other responsibilities.[22] More to the point, it has emerged as Putin's main agency for political control. The Cabinet of Ministers administers presidential policy; the AP helps the president formulate that policy, communicates it to the executive agencies, and monitors performance and compliance. It also houses figures who, like Peskov, have a close relationship with the president, including Vladislav Surkov (the political technologist widely assumed now to be managing strategy in Ukraine under the anodyne title of 'assistant to the president') and Yurii Ushakov, Putin's main foreign policy adviser.

The Presidential Administration is a powerful and complex agency under the presidential chief of staff, whose influence extends far beyond that envisaged in the laws framing it for the very reason that it dominates access to the president and likewise is the main conduit for his decisions. As such, it speaks with the authority of the Kremlin. Crucially, it also appears to be the institution through which requests for approval for major active measures operations appear to be routed, with a few exceptions largely involving personal relationships with the president. As described earlier, the attempted coup in Montenegro in 2016, for example, appears to have been enthusiastically overseen by Patrushev, who took it personally to Putin – but crucially not before informing the Presidential Administration, which thus still had a chance to weigh in.[23]

Until August 2016, the Presidential Administration was headed by Sergei Ivanov, a heavy-hitting veteran of the KGB and FSB, with a powerful reputation in the security and executive communities. His successor, Anton Vaino, is a rather less potent figure, so far at least, but in common with many of the key figures within the Presidential Administration, he is a foreign service veteran (and part of the 'MGIMO mafia' of alumni of the ministry's own university). The consensus among both Western Kremlin-watchers and Russian insiders and near-insiders is that he is focused on domestic policy and management issues, working with the first deputy chief of staff, Sergei Kirienko. Foreign affairs are instead part of the portfolio of the other first deputy chief of staff, Alexei Gromov. Another foreign ministry veteran, it is noteworthy that Gromov was placed under both EU and US sanctions for his role in the 2014 annexation of Crimea – while his superior at the time, Ivanov, is, as of the time of writing, only under EU sanction. It is also indicative that Gromov (a patron of Margarita Simonyan, head of RT)[24] appears to have responsibility for media affairs, even though Kirienko is point man for domestic politics.[25] Gromov may therefore be coordinating, possibly even commanding, the active measures campaign, given that it brings together foreign policy, media and other instruments.

To this end, he and the other key players (including Ushakov and Surkov) draw on key elements of the Presidential Administration of relevance to the active measures campaign, including six Presidential Administration departments and a series of Presidential Councils.[26] The Foreign Politics Department (UPVneshP) is especially involved with attempts to undermine the sanctions regime, for example, while the Department for Interregional Relations and Cultural Contacts with Foreign Countries (UPMKSZS) has a role in managing soft-power operations, including the work of *Rossotrudnichestvo*, the agency tasked with reaching out to ethnic Russians abroad. The Press and Information Directorate (UPSIP) manages contracts with the 'troll farms.'[27] The Presidential Council for Cossack Affairs plays a crucial role in not only mobilising Cossacks for domestic political purposes, but also encouraging pro-Kremlin groups abroad, such as the hundred Cossacks who turned up in Bosnia's turbulent Slavic Republika Srpska region as a visible demonstration of Moscow's support for local nationalists in 2014.[28]

Curating chaos

The Presidential Administration is the single most central institution in modern Russia, cocooning the president, curating his information flows and communicating his wishes. But it also has a unique breadth of responsibilities and unusual level of coherence. A number of Russian insiders with whom I have spoken has suggested that a combination of an organisational *esprit de corps* and a keen awareness of the privilege of their position (and by extension the desire not to lose it) tends to mean that it is far less fractious and cannibalistic than is often the case within Russian officialdom.

The AP is also a secretive structure, and even former staffers are often reluctant to discuss the detail of its work. A very tentative assessment is that, when active measures operations move beyond the level of local and agency initiative, it is the primary locus of coordination. Some actions are managed by the Security Council when they fall squarely within its remit. Others are driven by direct instruction from Putin, his personal entourage or are managed through other institutions. The general instrumentalisation of both business and the Russian Orthodox Church, for example, does not appear usually to be handled through the AP, although there are regular contacts between certain oligarchs and lesser 'minigarchs' such as Malofeev and the Presidential Administration leadership.

In some cases, the Presidential Administration is able essentially to dictate the official line, such as to the state-controlled media or, increasingly, the foreign ministry. In other cases, the relationship is more delicate. Dealing with the intelligence services, for example, appears to be something done not by AP departments, but by personal aides to key leadership figures such as Gromov. As one SVR veteran put it, 'at an operational level, we never dealt with them, nor did we get any instructions from them. That was something negotiated high above our heads, in the *banya* [bathhouse] or over drinks.'[29] However, given the concentration of power in the Presidential Administration, its capacity to task both collection operations and analyses from the intelligence community also reflects a powerful, indirect way of communicating if not instructions, then at least guidance as to the lines of action likely to be smiled upon. Likewise, the Ministry of Defence and General Staff are considered formally beyond being browbeaten by departments, but are instead handled at the managerial level.

The role of the Kremlin, mediated largely through the AP, is thus threefold. It is an inspiration for myriad bottom-up initiatives, setting direction and offering the hope of political and economic favour for those who deliver. It is a curator for initiatives, too, killing off some that appear dangerous or inconvenient, but more often encouraging and even taking over those that seem promising. Finally, it is the initiator for certain operations that address specific immediate or strategic needs. This is the essence of its diffuse, sometimes contradictory, often inefficient, but overall destructive and disruptive political war, one fought with a wide range of instruments, from the military and the media, to organised crime and oligarchs.

Notes

1 Online communication, March 2018.
2 This chapter draws heavily on Mark Galeotti, *Controlling Chaos: How Russia Manages Its Political War in Europe* (ECFR, 2017), and is used with permission.
3 Among many others, this formulation was used by Hillary Clinton on the *Rachel Maddow Show* on MSNBC, 18 September 2018.
4 n-tv, 26 January 2016.
5 Conversation in Moscow, January 2014.
6 Described by a former insider in 'Confessions of a (former) state TV reporter,' *Coda Story*, 25 April 2017, and corroborated by a number of informal conversations with other journalists.
7 Marlene Laruelle, 'The two faces of contemporary Eurasianism: an imperial version of Russian nationalism,' *Nationalities Papers*, 32, 1 (2004), pp. 115–136.
8 A study of the best-known *politologs*, the politically-oriented talking heads in the Russian media, found that in 2016, Dugin had fallen from 22nd in 2015 to 39th – see the results at www.regcomment.ru/investigations/reyting-rossiyskikh-politologov-po-upominaemosti-v-smi-v-2016-godu/ and www.regcomment.ru/investigations/reyting-rossiyskikh-politologov-po-upominaemosti-v-smi-v-2015-godu/.
9 Robert Beckhusen, 'Putin's "mad philosopher" is out of a job,' *War is Boring*, 29 June 2014.
10 Reuters, 19 October 2016.
11 RT, 1 July 2016.
12 BBC, 7 October 2016.
13 For useful background on this, see 'Balkan gambit: part 2. The Montenegro Zugzwang,' Bellingcat, 25 March 2017 www.bellingcat.com/news/uk-and-europe/2017/03/25/balkan-gambit-part-2-montenegro-zugzwang/.
14 Conversation in Sofia, March 2017.
15 This was confirmed by a former Presidential Administration staffer, a former Russian intelligence officer, and also several Western government officials working on Russia.
16 The first of the various reports comprising the dossier stated that the file on Trump was 'controlled by Kremlin spokesman PESKOV, directly on

PUTIN's orders.' See the full dossier at www.buzzfeed.com/kenbensinger/these-reports-allege-trump-has-deep-ties-to-russia.

17 Mark Galeotti, 'Free Sergei Lavrov!' *Foreign Policy*, 17 February 2016.

18 Conversation with foreign service officer, Moscow, January 2016.

19 Conversation in Moscow, April 2017.

20 'Vladimir Putin's man in the Balkans', *Politico*, 21 June 2017.

21 *Kommersant*, 28 October 2016; 'Serbia released Shishmakov at Patrushev's urging', CdM, 31 March 2018 www.cdm.me/english/serbia-released-shishmakov-patrushevs-urging/.

22 Its official establishment strength is just under 1,600, but this excludes staff seconded to the Presidential Administration from other agencies, including the intelligence and security services. This also excludes many of the support staff, such as the guards provided by the Federal Protection Service.

23 Patrushev's role was asserted by a Bulgarian intelligence officer in a conversation in Sofia in March 2017 and confirmed by a Russian intelligence veteran in Moscow, April 2017, who added the detail about how this was brought to Putin.

24 This is, ironically, something asserted both by the US intelligence community and Simonyan herself; see 'ODNI statement on declassified intelligence community assessment of Russian activities and intentions in recent U.S. elections,' 6 January 2017 https://icontherecord.tumblr.com/post/155494946443/odni-statement-on-declassified-intelligence and Simonyan's light-hearted response at https://sputniknews.com/russia/201701071049356450-sputnik-simonyan-report/.

25 RBK, 22 November 2016.

26 This is discussed in much greater detail in my *Controlling Chaos: How Russia Manages Its Political War in Europe* (ECFR, 2017).

27 This was suggested by both a Russian journalist who had looked at the St Petersburg operation, who was pretty bullish about the Presidential Administration's role, and also a former Presidential Administration staffer, who was more tentative, but came from a different department. Conversations, Moscow, January 2016 and May 2016, respectively.

28 Klix, 3 October 2014.

29 Conversation in Moscow, February 2014.

Part III
Weapons of the new wars

7 'Polite people'
Conventional military, unconventional uses

There are clear overlaps between the military's hybrid war and the administration's political war, especially in the weapons used in both. Russia does not believe wars in the main can be won with misdirection and disinformation, and has certainly not turned its back on its traditional sledgehammers of massed artillery fires, tank assaults and airpower.[1] However, alongside the sledgehammers, it has appreciated the need for forces that can also be scalpels, or perhaps stilettos, knives that can be palmed and kept hidden until the moment of strike. Furthermore, it sees its armed forces also as useful for coercive diplomacy and heavy-handed messaging. Russia's armed forces are therefore used to provide capabilities for the whole spread of options: from full-scale conflict, through the not-quite-war, preparatory stages of a hybrid war, all the way to pure political conflicts.

Heavy-metal diplomacy

It is striking how far the Russians seem to turn to brinkmanship and intimidating displays of military force. Buzzing NATO warships, sending bombers through the edges of European countries' airspace, and wargaming thinly veiled offensives against neighbours are part of a coherent, deliberate and sometimes even successful attempt to use military force – or its threat – as an undiplomatic diplomatic instrument and also a tool of information operations. Again, without claiming this is at all inspired by his thinking, the parallels with Messner's aggressive-diplomacy are striking.

For years until finally making a decision on a permanent deployment, for example, Moscow threatened to put nuclear-capable Iskander-M (SS-26) missiles in its Kaliningrad exclave. Then President Dmitrii Medvedev had warned in 2008 that this would happen if NATO went ahead with its planned siting of ballistic missile defence systems in Poland and the

Czech Republic.[2] Periodically, the 'Iskander card' was played whenever Moscow wanted to alarm the northern Europeans. Although the missile is primarily used for conventional precision strikes – as demonstrated in Georgia and Syria – the fact that it is nuclear-*capable* inevitably attracts particular attention from the public and politicians. The real significance was not military – which is relatively limited – but political.

This 'heavy metal diplomacy' (as I have described it elsewhere[3]) is another reflection of the way Russian thinking about information operations is a far broader concept than the West's, going beyond the usual realms of coercive diplomacy. In pursuit of Moscow's wider strategic goals of dividing, distracting and demoralising the West, the military has a distinct role. By seeming to make military confrontation more likely, and also by putting more demands on NATO burden-sharing agreements, forcing members to put more resources into protecting front-line states, military gestures and provocations help open divisions between countries more and less exercised by the supposed Eastern threat. For many in southern Europe, in particular, migration and terrorism flowing from the Middle East and North Africa seem a much more pressing concern. A 2015 Pew poll found only 48% of Spaniards, 47% of French and 40% of Italians expressing any willingness to honour their countries' commitments under NATO's Article 5 – which pledges mutual defence – in case of war with Russia.[4] As Estonian Foreign Minister Sven Mikser put it, Moscow is trying 'to break the solidarity of Western countries, sow insecurity and exploit windows when readiness to react to their provocative steps is lower.'[5]

While the primary purpose of Russian military exercises is still to build and maintain operational effectiveness, it is also clear that they are staged with an eye to Western opinion. In 2016, for example, 33,000 Russian troops wargamed seizing the Aland, Gotland and Bornholm islands in the Baltic Sea, territories of Finland, Sweden and Denmark, respectively. Even less subtle was the exercise in 2015, when Russian bombers simulated a nuclear attack on Bornholm, at a time when Denmark's political leadership were on the island. This was part of a coordinated political campaign triggered by debates in Denmark and Finland about potentially basing US missiles. In 2015, Russian ambassador Mikhail Vanin had warned that if this happened:

> Denmark would be part of the threat against Russia. It would be less peaceful and relations with Russia will suffer. It is, of course, your own decision – I just want to remind you that your finances and security will suffer.[6]

Likewise, in 2016 Putin rhetorically asked the Finns if they joined NATO: 'do you think we will continue to act in the same manner?' Russian troops had been pulled back from the Russo-Finnish border, he added, but 'do you think they will stay there?'[7]

Russia's demonstrable willingness to use force, in violation of international laws and norms, also means that it has particular authority when, as it so often does, it speaks the language of military threat. Moscow is certainly not reluctant to warn of military consequences, whether directly or through proxies. Such heavy-handed signalling is meant to intimidate its audience and make concessions – however distasteful – appear safer than confrontation. This can be part of major influence campaigns or immediate expressions of the Kremlin's displeasure. After London blamed Moscow for the murder of Russian defector Alexander Litvinenko in 2006, for example, the British noted a distinct increase in the number and frequency of Russian incursions into their airspace.[8]

Military moves can also be used as a strategic distraction. The launch of cruise missiles at Syrian targets in November 2015, for example, was in many ways a counter-productive and expensive piece of showmanship. In the immediate aftermath, Iran closed its airspace to further Russian launches. However, beyond generally demonstrating Russian capabilities, this attack was also likely in part to have been meant to distract from an upsurge in fighting in the Donbas, which involved Russian-supplied heavy weapons meant to have been withdrawn. In this way, the armed forces are also bit players in Moscow's geopolitical theatre.

Special forces, special missions

Whether they are called 'little green men' (the Western term) or 'polite people' (the Russian), the activities of the special forces who took Crimea in 2014,[9] and subsequently played a less overt but nonetheless crucial role in the Donbas,[10] have consolidated a belief for some that a central element of the purported new Russian way of war involves the deniable use of such forces. Not that this is really new; the Russians' traditional faith in *maskirovka* (disguise, or deception) makes such tactics fair game in the future, as they were in the past.[11] Besides which, although their gambit won them a few hours' confusion in Crimea (admittedly essential ones), precisely because it flew in the face of diplomatic, if not military, etiquette,[12] this is not a tactic easy to repeat. Estonian army commander General Riho Terras spoke for many frontline officers when he described the new lesson for NATO: when faced with armed men of uncertain provenance crossing your border, 'you should shoot the first one to appear.'[13]

The Russians have been building and honing scalable intervention capabilities that span the military and intelligence realms and that can be used effectively in deniable operations and in conjunction with political and economic instruments. First and foremost, these are the *Spetsnaz* ('Special Designation') special forces, but also elements of the VDV – air-assault troops or paratroopers – and the Naval Infantry marines. The *Spetsnaz* have been expanding, with a new brigade and regiment added to their strength and existing units brought to full establishment strength. As of late 2018, there are eight *Spetsnaz* brigades, each 1,000–1,500-strong,[14] the 25th Independent *Spetsnaz* Regiment at Stavropol and four Naval Reconnaissance Points, each roughly equivalent to a brigade. The paratroopers have their own 45th Independent Guards *Spetsnaz* Regiment. There is also a new Special Operations Forces Command (KSSO), formed in 2013, with some 2,000 operators, operating out of two hubs: the Senezh command centre at Solnechnogorsk, north-west of Moscow; and a barracks at Kubinka-2, west of the capital.[15]

There are thus some 17,000–18,000 *Spetsnaz*, but they are not all true special forces in the Western sense. Some 15–20% are still conscripts serving one-year terms (in theory these units were to be all-volunteer by the end of 2018, but as of the time of writing that seems unlikely), and *Spetsnaz* are trained for larger-scale operations, making them best considered expeditionary light infantry comparable with the US 75th Rangers or the UK's 16th Air Assault Regiment. The KSSO was formed precisely because the Russians came to appreciate the need for truly 'special' special forces, able to mount small, complex and deniable operations.[16] It is much more closely comparable to Western 'Tier One' special forces such as the USA's Delta and Britain's SAS. It is also supplemented by specialist elements attached to the other intelligence and security agencies, from the FSB's *Al'fa* anti-terrorist group to the SVR's highly-secretive *Zaslon* ('Barrier') group.[17]

Special forces are at once powerful and fragile. They are fast, flexible and can operate covertly and deniably. They cannot, though, seize and hold targets for long or last in pitched combat with regular forces. Their military role is often to be the 'tip of the spear,' in support of conventional military offensive operations. In Prague in 1968 and Kabul in 1979, for example, they seized airfields to allow other forces to deploy. In Crimea in 2014, they bottled up Ukrainian defenders and secured airfields and ports so that conventional units could be brought in. Beyond that, they conduct deep reconnaissance and rapid response. In Syria, for example, the KSSO spot for Russian airstrikes,[18] recover pilots and flight recorders from downed planes, and were used to rescue Russian military police surrounded by rebels in September 2017.[19]

Agents of chaos

Another traditional role for special forces is the disruption of the enemy's capabilities by cutting lines of supply and communications, targeting civil and military leaders and generally sowing chaos behind the battlefield with gun and bomb. In Afghanistan, the *Spetsnaz* did more than just seize the airport; the so-called 'Muslim Battalion,' made up of commandos of Central Asian appearance such that they were truly deniable, was also deployed to kill President Hafizullah Amin and paralyse the government. This remains a key role for the *Spetsnaz* today. However, as the politics behind modern warfare become all the more important, the Russians are also clearly looking to their commandos, especially the KSSO, for flexible operators fit to be used in political operations. They can create instability, which can in turn be used as a pretext for more overt and intensive intervention. As Gerasimov put it in his infamous 2013 article, there is scope for the 'open use of forces— often under the guise of peacekeeping and crisis regulation.'[20] This requires not simply smart, disciplined and well-trained special forces, it also demands a closer integration between them and planners and analysts with a better sense of the political environment in which they will operate. It is thus indicative that there appears since 2014 to have been a greater effort to unite what had been two relatively distinct wings of the GRU, the spies and analysts of the *Agentura* – 'agency,' as its intelligence side is informally known – and the battlefield assets of the *Spetsnaz*.

Another particular area of interest is the way that special forces can be used in information warfare. In Crimea, for example, they quickly seized the Simferopol internet exchange point (IXP) and targeted the telecommunications cables linking the peninsula with the mainland.[21] Physical control of the internet and telephone infrastructure gave Russia control of the information environment.[22] From this, wider lessons have been drawn about the information warfare value of seizing physical control of strategically significant internet infrastructure, including satellite stations, sub-sea cables, IXPs and more. After all, this permits the destruction, interdiction or modification of information passing through the infrastructure, a key facilitator for information dominance.

Finally, the *Spetsnaz* are heir to a tradition going back to the experience of the Soviet NKVD secret police in the Spanish Civil War and working with partisans in the Second World War. They are tasked with covertly training, mobilising and leading irregular proxy forces. This is currently especially relevant in the Donbas, where the GRU appears to have primary responsibility for marshalling the 'volunteers' – discussed below – and also both supporting and sometimes disciplining local militias. Ukrainian sources have claimed that at any one time, there are three to five *Spetsnaz* units in the Donbas, numbering at most a few hundred operators.[23] Much of their work is training militias, conducting reconnaissance and directing artillery strikes when government forces attack. However, they also have been credibly associated with operations to assert Moscow's control over the local warlords. There has been a spate of mysterious assassinations of especially inconvenient or independent militia commanders. These include Alexander 'Batman' Bednov and Alexei Mozgovoi in 2015, Arsen 'Motorola' Pavlov in 2016, a slew of lesser figures, and perhaps even Donetsk People's Republic Prime Minister Alexander Zakharchenko in 2018, although it is difficult sometimes to know exactly where to draw the line between political assassinations and murders stemming from personal and criminal feuds. The Russians inevitably blame these on the Ukrainian military. In this instance, Moscow appears willing to suggest that Kyiv fields commandos with ninja-like powers to infiltrate the Donbas, carry out assassinations and then sneak out without leaving a single shred of evidence. However, most of these killings are widely assumed to have been carried out by GRU or FSB *Spetsnaz*.[24]

Moscow's mercenaries

An additional hybrid variety of Russian military capacity is that of mercenary soldiers.[25] Moscow has dabbled with what could be called 'pseudo-mercenaries' in both the Donbas and Syria. Under Russian law, private military companies (ChVK), unlike regular security providers, are still banned. However, this has been bypassed by registering abroad units that appear essentially to have been established by the security agencies or the military. So far, the results have been mixed, but the potential to create military assets that are deniable and yet controlled and effective, as tools of the state, is something that has been recognised for some time. In 2011, Putin said such companies could further national interests without the direct involvement of the state and the following year First Deputy Prime Minister Dmitrii Rogozin again floated the idea.[26] Only in 2014, with the rapid deterioration of relations with the

West and the war in the Donbas did this get anywhere, though, even if ChVKs have still not been formally legalised.

The first, the Slavonic Corps, had a singularly unimpressive debut in Syria in 2013 and was soon disbanded, only to be succeeded by the rather more effective Wagner Group, whose roots were in GRU-curated 'volunteers' fighting in the Donbas.[27] Until around the beginning of 2017, Wagner – which performed a series of roles, from training and fire support to direct combat missions – was well-funded and -armed and little more than a deniable arm of the Russian military. In this case, the deniability was not so much towards the outside world as a Russia population clearly unwilling to see their boys die in this distant war. By using Wagner for the riskier missions, the government could maintain the fiction that Russia's role was essentially arm's-length, flying planes and distributing food, even though the clear majority of the mercenaries were Russian.

By the beginning of 2017, though, Wagner's job in Syria seemed largely done, and so the government in effect 'privatised' it, handing it over to one of Putin's trusted adhocrats, Evgenii Prigozhin. The flow of state funds seems to have dried up or at least dwindled, but Prigozhin was encouraged to find ways of monetising his military force. This he did first with a deal with the Syrian government whereby for five years Wagner would get 25% of the revenues from any oil and gas fields it recaptured,[28] and then branching out into security work in the Central African Republic. However, it is clear that the Kremlin reserves to itself the right to call on Wagner in the future. Furthermore, in 2018 it emerged that the defence ministry – which had blocked attempts to legalise mercenary companies in 2012 and 2018 – had established its own, called Patriot, which was operating in Syria.[29]

In the future, this may become more common a means of projecting Kremlin power. These forces may be marshalled by the FSB or the GRU, and may well as a result work to different agendas in-country. However, they presumably are being established to address the whole deniability-versus-effectiveness conundrum. After all, as the next chapter will explore, while the Russians are clearly happy to use militias, warlords, gangsters and other such thuggish non-state actors, these often are difficult to control – and of limited actual competence.

Notes

1 See, in particular, Jakob Hedenskog and Carolina Vendil Pallin (eds), *Russian Military Capability in a Ten-year Perspective – 2013* (FOI, 2013) and

Alexander Golts and Michael Kofman, *Russia's Military: Assessment, Strategy, and Threat* (Center on Global Interests, 2016).

2   Deutsche Welle, 19 October 2009.

3   Mark Galeotti, *Heavy Metal Diplomacy: Russia's Political Use of Its Military in Europe since 2014* (ECFR, 2016).

4   Pew Research Centre, *NATO Publics Blame Russia for Ukrainian Crisis, but Reluctant to Provide Military Aid*, June 2015.

5   Bloomberg, 1 December 2016.

6   *Jyllands-Posten*, 20 March 2015.

7   RT, 1 July 2016.

8   Andrew Foxall, *Close Encounters: Russian Military Intrusions into UK Air- and Sea Space Since 2005* (Henry Jackson Society, 2015).

9   See Alexey Nikolsky, 'Little, green, and polite: the creation of Russian special operation forces' and Anton Lavrov, 'Russian again: the military operation for Crimea,' in Colby Howard and Ruslan Pukhov (eds), *Brothers Armed: Military Aspects of the Crisis in Ukraine, 2nd edition* (EastView Press, 2015), pp. 124–131 and pp. 157–184.

10 See Igor Sutyagin, 'Russian forces in Ukraine,' RUSI Briefing Paper 9 (2015); Tor Bukkvoll, 'Russian special operations forces in Crimea and Donbas,' *Parameters*, 46, 2 (2016), pp. 13–21.

11 See, for example, V. A. Matsulenko, *Operativnaya maskirovka voisk* (Voenizdat: 1975); John Erickson, 'The Soviet military potential for surprise attack: surprise, superiority and time,' in Robert Pfaltzgraff, Uri Ra'anan and Warren Milberg (eds), *Intelligence Policy and National Security* (Palgrave Macmillan, 1981), pp. 74–81; Timothy Shea, 'Post-Soviet *maskirovka*, Cold War nostalgia, and peacetime engagement,' *Military Review*, 82, 3 (2002), pp. 63–67.

12 Roy Allison, 'Russian "deniable" intervention in Ukraine: how and why Russia broke the rules,' *International Affairs*, 90, 6 (2014), pp. 1255–1297.

13 Interviewed in the *Financial Times*, 13 May 2015.

14 The 2nd at Pskov, 3rd at Tolyatti, 10th at Molkino, 14th at Ussuriisk 16th at Moscow, 22nd at Stepnoi, 24th at Irkutsk and 100th at Mozdok.

15 Mark Galeotti, *Spetsnaz: Russia's Special Forces* (Osprey, 2015). See also Tor Bukkvoll, 'Military innovation under authoritarian government – the case of Russian special operations forces,' *Journal of Strategic Studies*, 38, 5 (2015), pp. 602–625.

16 *Izvestiya*, 27 November 2012; Dmitry Trenin, 'Russia's new tip of the spear,' *Foreign Policy*, 8 May 2013.

17 Vzglyad, 24 May 2014; TV-Zvezda, 22 October 2015.

18 RBK, 17 March 2016; *Voenno-promyshlennyi Kur'er*, 19 April 2016.

19 TV-Zvezda, 21 September 2017.

20 Valerii Gerasimov, 'Tsennost' nauki v predvidenii,' *Voenno-promyshlennyi kur'er*, 27 February 2013.

21 Ukrtelekom, 1 March 2014 www.ukrtelecom.ua/presscenter/news/official?id=120389.

22 Shane Harris, 'Hack attack. Russia's first targets in Ukraine: its cell phones and Internet lines,' *Foreign Policy*, 3 March 2014.
23 Based on conversations with Ukrainian security officials, December 2017.
24 *Kyiv Post*, 17 October 2016; *New York Times*, 8 February 2017; Meduza, 4 September 2018 https://meduza.io/en/feature/2018/09/04/why-was-the-separatist-leader-of-donetsk-assassinated.
25 *Voenno-promyslennyi kur'er*, 8 October 2014; RBC, 25 August 2016.
26 RIA Novosti, 13 April 2011; RIA Novosti, 19 September 2012.
27 Michael Weiss, 'The case of the Keystone Cossacks,' *Foreign Policy*, 21 November 2013; Fontanka, 29 March 2016; Mark Galeotti, 'Moscow's mercenaries in Syria,' War on the Rocks, 5 April 2016 https://warontherocks.com/2016/04/moscows-mercenaries-in-syria/.
28 *Washington Post*, 23 February 2018; *The Bell*, 27 February 2018.
29 Dozhd-TV, 5 July 2018; *Novaya gazeta*, 5 July 2018.

8 Impolite people

Militias and gangsters

> I won't deny that there were volunteers fighting there [in the Donbas],
> the best of the Russian army. I had several officers in my brigade who
> spent their vacation fighting for Novorossiya.
>
> (Igor 'Strelkov' Girkin, then defence minister of the
> unrecognised Donetsk People's Republic)[1]

The Russians, especially through the GRU, have been assiduous in using
deniable irregular forces, from the militias of Ukraine, Transnistria
and Georgia, to criminals. Of course, such non-state instruments
have been used by many other countries, from time to time. The initial US strategy in Afghanistan in 2001 was to rely on local fighters,
for example, and imperial powers have always depended on local auxiliaries and sepoys. However, for the Russians this has become more
than just an ad hoc situational option or a way of bolstering overt capacities; it is also a way of generating military capabilities that are also
political ones, operating across an active measures as well as a direct
warfighting spectrum.

Auxiliary forces can provide disruption, political cover, cannon fodder
and muscle for local proxy regimes. In Crimea, for example, while the
real task of securing the peninsula and blocking off Ukrainian garrisons
fell to elite Russian forces, 'local self-defence volunteers' drawn in some
cases from local organised crime groups loyal to Moscow's premier-
in-waiting Sergei Aksenov – himself gang-connected[2] – provided
much less professional but very visible gunmen to guard government
buildings (and often loot them). Since then, such forces have played
the primary role in the Donbas, supported by a mix of regular Russian
units, ad hoc collections of nationalists and adventurers, and everything
in between. These kinds of forces fall broadly into three categories,
each with their own distinctive strengths, weaknesses and modalities

of use: autonomous local militias; mercenaries and volunteers; and gangsters.

The Second Chechen War was to a considerable extent won thanks to 'Chechenisation' and the increasing use of warlords and militias to pit Chechen against Chechen. In Georgia, both Abkhaz and South Ossetian fighters played significant roles, not just as combatants but also as the political cover for the war, providing Moscow with a pretext for its actions. The rebel forces in the Donbas include defectors from the infamous Berkut special police and the Ukrainian military, organised crime groups seeing a chance to convert muscle into territorial power, street gangs, political movements and personal followings.[3] While generally overall control of such assets would be a GRU role (especially operating out of a regional headquarters in Rostov-on-Don, close to the border[4]), in Ukraine where the FSB also has an historic stake, this can be a disputed issue. However, as is discussed below, the level of control the Kremlin can actually assert is sometimes limited, one of the costs of deniability.

Volunteers and mercenaries

Most of these conflicts are framed in terms of defending Russians or a kindred ethnic minority against terror and oppression. As a result, they also attract Russian fighters who are officially operating wholly outside Kremlin control. A classic example would be the Cossacks. They have been used as deniable government assets since well before the Putin era, whether in the anti-Jewish pogroms of late tsarism or the Transnistria secession war of 1992.[5] Under Putin, though, a particular alliance has formed and Cossacks fought in Chechnya, Georgia and now the Donbas.[6] Beyond them, there are individual Russian soldiers 'volunteering' in the Donbas while 'on leave,' or members of paramilitary and violent groups such as the Night Wolves motorcycle gang.[7] These mercenaries, nationalists and adventurers are often of questionable military value but considerable enthusiasm, and also useful political-propaganda tools, demonstrating alleged popular support. It is also difficult often to unpick who is participating in the conflict because of genuine zeal and who is there on secret orders. Given that it is an offence under Russian military law to fight in an unofficial capacity, one would expect many of those 'vacationers' to have subsequently been arrested and tried. Yet the infrequency with which this actually happened suggests at least a deliberate turning of a blind eye and probably that this is just a fiction to explain sending trained soldiers into the conflict.

These categories are, of course, broad and overlapping. An interesting twist on this model was provided by the Vostok Battalion, a force predominantly of Chechen soldiers, leavened with Ossetians and other volunteers from the Caucasus. It was formed around a core of veterans from the original battalion, Chechens who fought for the GRU in the Second Chechen War and the Georgian War before being disbanded. The GRU reformed the battalion in 2014 and sent it into Donetsk, where as its first act it seized the rebel headquarters in what appears to have been a pointed reminder that Moscow was in charge. In short order, a Ukrainian, Alexander Khodakovskii was appointed to head the battalion and many of the Chechens were withdrawn, replaced by locals. In this respect, Vostok was a thinly-deniable Russian force that then became a local militia, bridging two varieties of paramilitary.[8]

Either way, it is important to note, though, that there are severe limitations to such units. In some cases, they are hard to control. Ramzan Kadyrov, leader of Chechnya, whose 'Kadyrovtsy' served both his father and then him, helped crush the rebels in that turbulent republic, but in the process became its virtually independent ruler, funded by the federal budget.[9] The more deniable the force, typically the more tenuous the control. As independent actors, they can and do try to make Moscow accommodate their political and economic agendas, from providing subsidies and payoffs through to shaping policy. They are also frequently undisciplined, and this also can create reputational costs, something most starkly visible with the shooting down of Malaysian airliner MH17 over the Donbas, by local militias using a Russian-supplied SA-17 Buk missile, yet probably not on Russian orders.[10]

Second, they are often of at best indifferent quality: there is an almost inverse relationship between deniability and effectiveness. In the Donbas, the conflict really began in April 2014, with the bulk of insurgent operations carried out by locals, supported by a relative handful of Russian paramilitaries. Only in late May, as Ukrainian government forces and their irregular allies looked likely to triumph on the battlefield, did Moscow begin seriously to infiltrate its own conventional forces into the conflict, along with such elements as Vostok. By August, a new approach had been adopted, and Russian regular contingents including armoured units and paratroopers were being deployed.[11] Although Moscow continued to deny its role, and terrorist and other non-military attacks were being launched inside the rest of Ukraine regularly, the true 'hybrid' phase of the conflict thus lasted only a few months, and ended precisely because methods and forces effective in creating chaos were ineffective in harnessing it.[12]

Gangsters as assets

> I must say that I don't like the term hybrid warfare, it sounds far too nice ... I would like to bring your attention to CRIMINALITY as an aspect of the new hybrid war.
>
> (Aivar Jaeski, deputy director, NATO STRATCOM Centre of Excellence)[13]

The Russian state is especially willing to use organised crime as a source of resources, operational capacity and intelligence.[14] Spanish investigative magistrate José Grinda Gonzalez noted back in 2010 that the Kremlin was willing to use gangs 'to do whatever the [government of Russia] cannot acceptably do as a government.'[15] This should hardly be a surprise, given the close relationships that have emerged inside the country between underworld, business and politics. The anarchy of the 1990s saw a particular form of gangster capitalism emerge, and when Putin came to power in 2000, he was able to draw on his own experiences dealing with the Tambovskaya gang in St Petersburg during his time as the city's deputy mayor, to enforce a new social contract with the gangsters.[16] In essence, they were given a degree of freedom to thieve and extort, so long as they posed no direct or overt challenge to the state. During the Second Chechen War, for example, Moscow was able to persuade Chechen criminals not to support their rebel compatriots on pain of retribution. Over time, in line with Putin's creation of a mobilisation state, a negative relationship has turned into a more positive one. Rather than simply setting the boundaries of the criminals' acceptable behaviour, increasingly it has instead turned to them to carry out specific actions.[17]

This is especially evident abroad, notably in Europe, where the spread of Russian-based organised crime networks and their close connections with local gangs provides a wide range of opportunities. After all, Russian-based criminal networks are responsible for around one-third of the heroin on Europe's streets, a significant amount of non-European people trafficking, as well as most illegal weapons imports.[18] Putin's 'Crimintern' has become much more problematic since 2014, in a variety of ways. First of all, while Russia's security agencies have built up formidable cyberintelligence capabilities, they still turn, from time to time, to criminal hackers, induced by payment, threat or simply appeals to their patriotism. This kind of 'outsourcing' is a response to the way opportunities in the cyber realm are still outstripping the expansion of state capabilities, although as with militias and warlords, deniability and the opportunity to pick up 'off the shelf' assets often come at the expense of competence and discipline. Major operations such as those surrounding the 2016 US presidential elections are the responsibility of state agents, but many of the more general intrusions meant to disrupt and identify weaknesses appear more likely to be the work of freelancers. These include the 2010 hack of NASDAQ's central systems and smaller scale sabotage such as the defacing of websites perceived as 'Russophobic' or the persecution of individuals likewise considered hostile.[19] They also provide 'surge capacity' for major operations such as the attacks on Estonia in 2007 and Georgia in 2008 – which overwhelmed and crashed websites and servers by flooding them with traffic – as well as ongoing cyber disruption in Ukraine. Putin's disingenuous claim that the US electoral hack could have been the result of individual initiative, that if hackers 'are patriotically minded, they start making their contributions—which are right, from their point of view—to the fight against those who say bad things about Russia,' was a particular call to arms for such individuals.[20]

There are many other ways criminals can also be of use. People smugglers can help move agents across borders, as likely happened when the wanted Russian agent known as Christopher Metsos dropped out of sight in Cyprus in 2010.[21] Other times, it is goods and weapons that need to be moved. As Russia looks to support paramilitary groups such as the Hungarian National Front, and the agitators who took part in the Moscow-backed attempted coup in Montenegro in 2016, the capacity of criminals to smuggle weapons and equipment is becoming significant.[22] Even more directly, over and above their value in militias, criminals can and do kill. Again, on the one hand, it is clear that high-profile operations such as the murder of former FSB officer Alexander Litvinenko in 2006 and attempted killing of ex-GRU officer Sergei Skripal in 2018, both in the UK, were handled by professional intelligence officers. On the other hand, a number of lower-profile killings, notably of supporters of Chechen and other North Caucasus militants in Istanbul and Vienna, have been connected to organised crime groups that would appear to have no evident motive.[23] For example, Nadim Ayupov, one of the killers of three Chechens in Istanbul, was a member of a Moscow-based gang specialising in car theft.[24] The Turkish authorities believe the criminals to have been engaged by the FSB.[25]

Perhaps most importantly, though, crime pays, and criminal networks thus have both funds and ways of laundering and moving them without leaving a trail back to Moscow. This appears to be a growing source of what the Russians call *chernaya kassa* or 'black account' untraceable money that can be used in support of political warfare operations. This especially came to light in 2014, when

Estonian Kapo (Security Police) officer Eston Kohver was kidnapped by an FSB *Spetsnaz* team as he about to meet an informant. He was bundled back to Russia and then convicted on trumped-up espionage charges. Kohver had been investigating cross-border cigarette smuggling, and it emerged that the criminals in question were being allowed across the Russian border unhindered in return for some basic intelligence gathering and a cut of the profits. This was not going into some officer's pocket, but apparently to provide operational funds in Europe with no apparent Russian connection. Money is power, and the spies are eager to build up the *chernaya kassa* as one of their key weapons of political war.

Notes

1 In a video summarised by *The Interpreter*, 13 September 2014 www.interpretermag.com/is-colonel-strelkov-making-a-comeback-or-has-he-been-tamed/.

2 *Der Spiegel*, 25 March 2014; Taras Kuzio, 'Crime and politics in Crimea,' oDR, 14 March 2014 www.opendemocracy.net/od-russia/taras-kuzio/crime-and-politics-in-crimea-Aksyonov-Goblin-Wikileaks-Cables.

3 Mark Galeotti, 'Crime and Crimea: criminals as allies and agents,' RFE/RL, 3 November 2014 www.rferl.org/a/crimea-crime-criminals-as-agents-allies/26671923.html.

4 UNIAN, 10 October 2014.

5 This was confirmed by a former GRU officer in conversation in February 2016.

6 See Tomáš Baranec, 'Russian Cossacks in service of the Kremlin: recent developments and lessons from Ukraine,' *Russian Analytical Digest*, 153 (25 July 2014), pp. 9–12; Christopher Gilley, 'Otamanshchyna?: the self-formation of Ukrainian and Russian warlords at the Beginning of the twentieth and twenty-first centuries,' *Ab Imperio*, 3 (2015), pp. 73–95.

7 The Estonians, for example, have openly labelled the Night Wolves a security threat. *Eesti Päevaleht*, 27 June 2013.

8 Claire Bigg, 'Vostok Battalion, a powerful new player in eastern Ukraine,' RFE/RL, 30 May 2014.

9 Tomáš Šmíd and Miroslav Mareš, ' "Kadyrovtsy": Russia's counter-insurgency strategy and the wars of paramilitary clans,' *Journal of Strategic Studies*, 38, 5 (2015), pp. 650–677.

10 JIT, 'Update in criminal investigation MH17 disaster,' 24 May 2018 www.om.nl/onderwerpen/mh17-vliegramp/persbijeenkomst-24/narrative-conference/@103183/update-criminal/.

11 See Michael Kofman, 'Russian hybrid warfare and other dark arts,' War on the Rocks, 11 March 2016 http://warontherocks.com/2016/03/russian-hybrid-warfare-and-other-dark-arts/.

12 Sergey Minasyan, '"Hybrid" vs. "Compound" war: lessons from the Ukraine conflict,' *PONARS Eurasia Policy Memo* No. 401 (2015).
13 Aivar Jaeski, 'Hybrid warfare on the rise: a new dominant military strategy?' NATO STRATCOM COE, 24 November 2015 (capitals in the original).
14 Mark Galeotti, *Crimintern: How the Kremlin Uses Russia's Criminal Networks in Europe* (ECFR, 2017).
15 According to a US diplomatic cable released by Wikileaks. See www.theguardian.com/world/us-embassy-cables-documents/247712.
16 Karen Dawisha, *Putin's Kleptocracy* (Simon & Schuster, 2014), pp. 104–162.
17 I explore the rise of organised crime in Russia and its evolving relationship with the state in my *The Vory: Russia's Super Mafia* (Yale University Press, 2018).
18 Heroin data from conversations with Europol analyst, January 2016; human trafficking from Eurostat and Interpol analyses. Both the human trafficking and firearms figures explicitly exclude trafficking within Europe, although some Russian-based groups are also involved in these businesses.
19 See, for example, the activities of 'CyberBerkut' attacking journalists such as Bellingcat's Elliot Higgins involved in trying to identify the real perpetrators of the Malaysian Airlines MH17 shoot-down over the Donbas; *International Business Times*, 17 December 2015.
20 *New York Times*, 1 June 2017.
21 'Metsos' was one of the deep-cover 'illegals' unmasked in the USA that year. The suggestion he was smuggled out of Cyprus by criminals came from separate conversations with US counter-intelligence officers and an analyst with Interpol. Cyprus has long been something of a Russian criminal playground.
22 *New York Times*, 24 December 2016; Balkan Insight, 21 February 2017.
23 BBC, 13 December 2016; *Der Spiegel*, 23 June 2010.
24 'Have Russian hitmen been killing with impunity in Turkey?' BBC, 13 December 2016 www.bbc.co.uk/news/magazine-38294204.
25 *Hurriyet Daily News*, 19 February 2014.

9 Invisible people

The 'warriors of the hidden battlefield'

> For the past ten years, the West has been trying to bring us down, and
> we [intelligence officers] have been the front-line soldiers.
>
> (A recently retired former SVR officer)[1]

Russia's intelligence agencies are central to the country's geopolitical
campaigns, reflecting both their privileged position within decision-
making circles and also the essentially wartime mentality they and Putin
share. They are not simply or primarily gatherers of information: active
measures from blackmail and subversion to assassination and sabotage
are central to their mission. In the West, we have historically failed to
understand them, in particular because we assume some comparability
with our own. In fact, the best parallels are wartime sabotage and diver-
sion services such as the Second World War's US Office of Strategic
Services and Britain's Special Operations Executive. Russia's intelligence services, after all, operate on a permanent wartime footing. To
a considerable extent this pre-dates Putin. In his 1999 autobiography,
former spymaster Evgenii Primakov wrote: 'All of us in the leadership
of the Foreign Intelligence Service realized perfectly well that the concept of the enemy would not disappear with the end of the "Cold War",'
not least because the West was trying to 'disrupt the trend towards the
increasing rapprochement with the Russian Federation' of the other
post-Soviet states.[2] In other words, even before Putin's rise there has
been an assumption among many within the intelligence and security
community that the West was working to keep Russia isolated and
weakened. The implications of this mindset are serious,[3] especially as it
is shared by a Kremlin that appears to heed the spooks much more than
its own diplomats.[4]

The organs

In Soviet times, there were essentially only two agencies: the Committee of State Security (KGB), handling everything from foreign espionage to domestic security; and the Main Intelligence Directorate (GRU) of the General Staff, responsible for military intelligence. The KGB was powerful and willing to use espionage, destabilisation and subversion, but was also tightly controlled by a political leadership ultimately committed to the status quo. Under Boris Yeltsin in the 1990s, the state was weak, but the intelligence agencies doubly so. Nonetheless, initial plans for a comprehensive reform of the intelligence community soon foundered, as Yeltsin surrendered to resistance from KGB veterans in his circle.

The agencies began to be revived during Putin's first terms as president, but his initial policy was one of pragmatic accommodation with the West. This changed, and even by 2010, the British Security Service (MI5) was warning: 'The threat from Russian espionage continues to be significant and is similar to the Cold War ... the number of Russian intelligence officers in London is at the same level as in Soviet times.'[5] The challenge has only increased, with security services across the West noting that the Russians are operating with increasing confidence and aggressiveness.

There are three main agencies operating internationally. The Federal Security Service (FSB) is the first among equals, a domestic security agency that has increasingly expanded its remit into international operations and offensive and defensive cybersecurity. The Foreign Intelligence Service (SVR) and the GRU (since 2010 technically known as the GU[6]) are the principal foreign intelligence agencies. As noted above, this intelligence and security community may look broadly familiar to Westerners, with the same broad split as between America's Federal Bureau of Investigation, Central Intelligence Agency and Defense Intelligence Agency, respectively. However, there are institutional and cultural characteristics that, combined with the nature of decision-making within the Russian system, mean that these agencies and the 'new nobility' who work in them – as former FSB director Nikolai Patrushev called them[7] – have a distinctive operational culture of their own.

They are not the power behind the throne in Moscow. They are divided within and between themselves, competitive at times to the point of cannibalism, and as dependent on Putin as any other elements of this highly personalised system. They are also often poorly tasked and poorly managed, set unrealistic objectives, granted extensive latitude for corruption and encouraged to compete. This competition can be a strength. It means the agencies are often aggressive, imaginative and entrepreneurial. It also means a degree of planned redundancy. In theory, it should provide multiple, independent perspectives. As journalist Yuliya Latynina put it: 'The war between the security services is our "separation of powers." Some of them whisper into the president's right ear, others into the left.'[8]

In practice, though, there are serious drawbacks. The urge for quick results often encourages agencies to seize the low-hanging fruit and poach on each other's turf. In 2014, for example, GRU officer Colonel Viktor Ilyushin was expelled from France after seeking to gather compromising information – *kompromat* in Russian parlance – on then President François Hollande, the kind of political operation that would usually be an SVR or even FSB responsibility.[9] Meanwhile, in the Baltic States and Nordic Europe, the FSB has steadily expanded its political operations to rival the SVR and GRU.[10]

More to the point, the need to please a president who has appeared increasingly intolerant of bad news and rival perspectives undermines the integrity of the gathering and analytic processes, which are vital if intelligence is to be of true value. As one former Russian intelligence officer told me, they had learned that 'you do not bring bad news to the tsar's table.'[11] Thus, too often, they tell the president what they think he wants to hear rather than what he needs to know. The result can be disastrously poor decision-making, based on the rational assessment of unreliable information. The Donbas intervention, for example, seems to reflect guidance that Kyiv would quickly realise that it could not escape Moscow's orbit and capitulate. One Western diplomat suggested to me that Putin's apparent belief in some more outré conspiracy theories – such as that the Ukrainian Maidan revolution was a CIA plot – probably stem from FSB briefings, 'which seem as much culled from the press and the more lunatic think-tanks as from actual intelligence.'[12]

There are distinct differences in the cultures of the agencies. The FSB, as befits essentially a domestic security agency in an authoritarian regime, appears politically oriented and unused to external constraints (and hence especially corrupt). The SVR, most of whose case officers work under diplomatic cover, has internalised at least a little of the foreign service's desire to avoid international incidents. The GRU is a military service, where taking risks and accomplishing the mission take precedence: as one former officer put it, 'not all of us were *Spetsnaz*, but we like to think we all are like *Spetsnaz*.'[13] However, the emphasis across all the agencies on coercive methods, active measures, taking chances and risking international opprobrium reflects a wartime mindset they seem to share. Even before the worsening of relations with the West, they appear genuinely to have felt that Russia was under serious, even existential, threat, which demanded extreme responses, making them forward-leaning, believing in the main that action was better than inaction.

The three 'p's

Overall, while still intelligence-gathering services, they also perform three key roles in terms of more active operations: providing pretexts; creating preconditions; and acting as paralysers. In the age of 'lawfare' (the deliberate abuse of legal processes to justify aggression or prevent responses to it) and information operations, it becomes especially important to create narratives supportive of Russian activities. The intelligence agencies are useful for creating pretexts for operations. They were, for example, crucial in encouraging, directing and supporting South Ossetian militias to launch the attacks that provoked a Georgian response in 2008, allowing Moscow to claim it was acting to defend its own peacekeepers and civilian populations. The potential penetration of Russophones in the Baltic States primarily by the FSB, and the encouragement of protest at their treatment, could conceivably be a future similar excuse for some kind of intervention, although this seems increasingly unlikely. After all, while many of them have their grievances, especially over native-language requirements, few show any enthusiasm to swap citizenship of a rule-of-law-based EU state for the Russian Federation.[14]

When some kind of offensive or political operation is launched, the agencies can be powerful force multipliers used to create preconditions for success. In the case of the annexation of Crimea, for example, not only did the FSB and GRU help scout out the battlespace and mobilise the 'self-defence volunteers,' but they also helped disrupt Ukrainian command and control, to ensure no coherent or timely response. Likewise, they appear to have been behind terrorist acts and cyberattacks against Kyiv in support of operations in the Donbas.[15] This follows an existing pattern. Georgia before the 2008 war saw killings and terrorist attacks aimed less at specific individuals than at creating a climate of fear and insecurity.[16] This is meant to undermine public and political will, and to support a Russian narrative that these countries are falling into anarchy. Where guns or bombs are not called for, sometimes a computer virus or dirty tricks will work. In Ukraine, for example, the FSB stands accused of being behind the poisoning of Viktor Yushchenko during the 2004 presidential elections and it reportedly leaked a forged document meant to derail a gas deal between Kyiv and Turkmenistan.[17]

Finally, the intelligence agencies have a significant role in strategic information operations to paralyse and disrupt those external forces that seek to block Russian moves (as Chekinov and Bogdanov noted). Dividing and distracting NATO and the EU is a political priority, and the agencies work alongside the Ministry of Foreign Affairs and the state-controlled media to this end. Estonia's Security Police, for example, accuse the FSB of not only penetrating the Russian-speaking population but also of seeking to suborn and corrupt politicians and opinion-formers in general.[18] This is a claim echoed elsewhere in the Baltics and, indeed, across Europe as a whole. Close ties between the SVR and *Rossotrudnichestvo*, the Federal Agency for the Commonwealth of Independent States, Compatriots Living Abroad and International Humanitarian Cooperation, attest to a particular interest in using Russian diaspora communities as potential instruments, even if it is open to question just how useful a tactic this will prove.[19] Through such fronts, the intelligence agencies support political and other movements sympathetic to or simply useful for Moscow. This has long been practised in countries Russia regards as within its sphere of influence. For example, the FSB interfered in Moldovan politics by backing populist Renato Usatii in 2014.[20] However, the SVR and FSB are now especially active in Europe via the unwitting organisations they support, whoever could be usefully disruptive, be they separatists, nationalists and anti-federalists, ultra-leftists or ultra-rightists.

The old cliché that when you have a hammer every problem looks like a nail is more than a little appropriate here. Under Vladimir Putin, the security and intelligence community has done very well, with steadily growing budgets, ever-broader powers, and the indulgence and support of a president who regards them fondly as his greatest support base. That gives them a strong political voice and also a reason to lobby for a significant role in Russian strategy. Both hybrid and political war grant this community a particularly central role, and so they are inevitably among their advocates. And so, in a circular process, capacity shapes policy, and policy shapes investment in further capacity.

Notes

1 Conversation, Moscow, January 2016.
2 Evgenii Primakov, *Gody v bol'shoy politike* (Sovershenno sekretno, 1999), pp. 133, 135.

3 I explore this more in my 2016 report for the ECFR, *Putin's Hydra: Inside Russia's Intelligence Services.*
4 Mark Galeotti, 'Free Sergei Lavrov!,' *Foreign Policy*, 17 February 2016.
5 *Guardian*, 29 June 2010.
6 The Main Intelligence Directorate of the General Staff simply became the Main Directorate, but this is such an anodyne term, especially as there are other main directorates, that in practice even Russian security insiders still talk of the GRU.
7 *Komsomolskaya Pravda*, 20 December 2000.
8 *Novaya gazeta*, 11 October 2007.
9 *Le Nouvel Observateur*, 24 July 2014.
10 For example, Latvia's Constitutional Protection Bureau's 2016 report specifically notes the use of blackmail and coercion by the FSB to recruit assets. 'Several cases of Russian intelligence agents forcing Latvian residents to cooperate with them noticed last year,' LETA, 29 March 2016.
11 Conversation, Moscow, 2014.
12 Conversation, Moscow, 2015.
13 Conversation, Moscow, 2014.
14 Especially among younger Russophones, the level of integration in Estonia – the front-line state – has been steadily increasing, for example, according to a 2015 survey. 'Young Estonian Russians feeling more integrated,' Estonian Public Broadcasting, 15 June 2015.
15 Taras Kuzio, 'Ukraine reignites,' *Foreign Affairs*, 25 January 2015.
16 The US government cable 'Russian active measures in Georgia' of 20 July 2007 gives an especially good account of operations conducted by both the GRU and FSB to provoke President Saakashvili into making the first move https://wikileaks.org/plusd/cables/07TBILISI1732_a.html.
17 Andrei Soldatov, 'The true role of the FSB in the Ukrainian crisis,' *Moscow Times*, 15 April 2014.
18 Estonian World Review, 21 April 2011.
19 See, for example, Orysia Lutsevych, *Agents of the Russian World: Proxy Groups in the Contested Neighbourhood* (Chatham House, 2016).
20 *Ziarul de gardă* , 27 November 2014.

10 Everyone else
The mobilisation state

> Listen: we engage in foreign policy the way we engage in war, with every means, every weapon, every drop of blood. But like in war, we depend on both the strategy of the general in the High Command, and the bravery and initiative of the soldier in the trench.
>
> (Russian former diplomat, 2017)[1]

As already noted, under Vladimir Putin, traditional Russian and even Soviet notions of the supremacy of the interests of the state have led to the creation of not so much a totalitarian but a 'mobilisation state.'[2] As Putin himself put it: 'It is only by mobilising all the resources at our disposal, both administrative and financial, that we will be able to get results.'[3] This is not totalitarianism. The government is willing – within certain bounds – to accept the presence of civil society, a free press, independent economic activity and even some limited and managed political pluralism. However, in keeping with its general philosophical belief that it is at (political) war and faces an existential cultural and political threat from the West, it reserves to itself the right to conscript any individual or organisation when it feels the need. As a result, it is worth dwelling on just how bewilderingly broad an array of different kinds of ostensibly civil players are involved in its political warfare, sometimes constantly, sometimes episodically, over and above government agencies such as the military, foreign ministry and intelligence services.

Of course, as with all aspects of contemporary Russia's playbook, this is by no means wholly new. Coercive diplomacy, the support of useful political groups and individuals in other countries, propaganda and economic leverage have long been accepted instruments of geopolitics. Putin's Russia is, rather, distinctive in the scale of their use, and also in the integration of state and theoretically non-state actors, regardless of legal status, role or ideology.

Information and disinformation

> Q: OK, why does the country need [RT] all? Why should I, as a taxpayer, support you?
> A: Well, for the same kind of reasons why the country needs a defence ministry. Why do you, as a taxpayer, need that? ... the defence ministry isn't fighting anyone at the moment, but it's ready for defence. So are we.
>
> (Interview with Margarita Simonyan, head of RT TV network, 2012)[4]

Much has already been written and said about the Russians' use of their own and foreign media, as well as the global realms of social media, to press their own positions, contest others' and generally seek to undermine foreign unity and will.[5] For my purposes here, it is therefore not necessary to do more than indicate that this is an important aspect of the overall political war campaign, even if the actual impact is often hard to ascertain and is at least sometimes extremely limited. Russian TV, still the way most Russians get their news, is directly controlled by the state or else heavily influenced by it. It pumps out often ludicrous propaganda at home, with such treats as the claim that former Swedish Foreign Minister Carl Bildt fomented the Ukrainian revolution as revenge for Russo-Swedish wars of the fifteenth to eighteenth centuries.[6] However, it is the extensive array of overt and covert state propaganda arms operating abroad such as the Sputnik news agency (publishing in 30 languages) and RT TV foreign news service (broadcasting in English, Arabic and Spanish) that attract particular opprobrium. Then there is an array of covert ways that Moscow messages the world, not least the so-called 'troll farms' such as the infamous St Petersburg-based Internet Research Agency (since relocated and rebranded).[7] Here, paid workers spend their shifts faithfully placing online posts and comments according to strict instructions from the management, sometimes advertising commercial products and services, but largely working to a political agenda, infecting social media with a range of divisive and contentious talking points and toxic memes.

However, much of the pro-Russian – or more often Russia-useful – content online comes not from such outlets so much as self-motivated individual internet trolls faithfully redistributing Russian talking points, excoriating Kremlin critics and generally jamming the online discussion sphere with chaff. This speaks to a wider and often worrying successful Russian campaign to suborn and support appropriate opinion-shapers, from journalists and public figures to think-tanks and political parties.[8] Sometimes, these are politically sympathetic to the Kremlin, often not so much because of an informed enthusiasm for all things Russian, as out of a sense of shared animosity, whether to the US, liberal values or their own governments. Others are essentially recruited agents, or acting out of personal self-interest, whether as paid lobbyists or for other direct gain. There are also the so-called 'useful idiots' (after a term mistakenly ascribed to Lenin, who never actually seems to have used it) who may not even realise whose side they are taking, but retweet and magnify eye-catching stories that conform to their own biases.

As with all such political campaigns, where possible, various forms of information warfare are combined. In 2014, for example, Russian media reported that Dmitrii Yarosh, leader of the Ukrainian ultra-nationalist Right Sector organisation, had used social media to ask Chechen rebels to stage terrorist attacks within Russia.[9] Yarosh later stated that his account had been hacked in order to place the appeal, but the effect on public opinion both in Russia and Ukraine had already been substantial, in an operation that appears to have involved hackers, journalists and trolls together. This is made easier by the use of 'false-flag' active measures operations. When alleged Russian hackers took control of France's TV5 television channel in April 2015, for example, they played not Moscow's propaganda, but jihadist messages supposedly from the Islamic State's 'CyberCaliphate.' The goal was to alarm, to invigorate the nationalist right and to turn attention towards the Middle East.[10] The aim, after all, is essentially to question the country's support for Western policies and institutions, as far as possible by playing to traditional values, rather than replace those views with any coherent alternative.

That said, the role of these information operations is often misunderstood and over-stated, perhaps precisely because it is by definition public, and also because it is easy to assume causation where it might not exist. Furthermore, the 'hybrid-industrial complex' of 'mythbusters' and 'information warriors' in the West, pundits and NGOs that have hurriedly reinvented themselves as inquisitors scouring the ether for Russian sympathisers and 'useful idiots,' has a vested interest in talking up the threat and thus maintaining the flow of grants and fees on which they rely. It is not, after all, as though every Eurosceptic or even NATO-sceptic individual was made that way by Russian propaganda. The generalised crisis of legitimacy gripping the West, and the populist wave it has engendered, is essentially home-grown; Moscow at best encourages and benefits from it. What Christopher Paul and Miriam Matthews called with alliterative verve the 'firehose of falsehoods' seeks to wash away certainty and consensus.[11] Nonetheless, disinformation, the spread of often false or distorted news, and a deluge of alternative opinions meant to drown out the realities are undoubtedly central elements of the current political war.

All businesses big and small

If today's Russian style of contestation is described as hybrid war for the way it blends overt and covert, kinetic and political, then Moscow must also be considered the master of 'hybrid business,' of developing commercial enterprises – legal and illegal – that make money but, at the same time, whether technically private concerns or not, can be used for the Kremlin's purposes.[12] State-owned or state-dominated corporations such as Vnesheconombank (100% government-owned), Rosneft (50%) and Gazprom (50.23%) have long been used as instruments of state policy, from channelling resources to projects that the Kremlin considers a priority, to exerting pressure through limiting energy supplies. However, a crucial aspect to the mobilisation state is that the government can and will from time to time ask favours that are clearly requests that cannot be refused. As part of the price of doing business without potential hindrance, or in the hope of future benefit, companies may be expected to provide funding for foreign political parties or campaigns, contribute to useful causes or otherwise dance to the Kremlin's tune.

Acting notionally on their own initiative, they have been used to provide financial support to political and social movements Moscow deems convenient, from Marine Le Pen's anti-EU *Front nationale* in France (which received a €9 million loan from a bank run by a close Putin ally[13]) to the Czech Republic's Russophile President Miloš Zeman (whose 2013 election was partially bankrolled by the local head of the Russian oil company Lukoil, allegedly as a personal donation[14]). They are also crucial in the outright co-optation of local figures in the West. Estonia's former President Toomas Ilves calls this '*Schröderizatsiya,*' after the lucrative employment of former German Chancellor Gerhard Schröder by Gazprom and his role as one of the highest-profile *Putinverstehers* or 'Putin-understanders' advocating the Kremlin's interests abroad.

This is not always or necessarily simply a grudging response to a quiet command from Moscow. Businesses and wealthy Russians are often also enthusiastic and self-motivated participants in active measures, out of conviction or ambition. Investment banker Konstantin Malofeev, for example, stands accused by the European Commission and the US of being a prime mover behind the seizure of Crimea and destabilisation of the Donbas.[15] He appears to have bankrolled active measures operations in Crimea preparing the ground for annexation and reportedly admits he was behind the deployment into the Donbas of Igor 'Strelkov'

Girkin, the Russian operator who boasts of being the man who 'pulled the trigger' on that undeclared war.[16] He was also the former employer of Alexander Boroday, first premier of the self-proclaimed Donetsk People's Republic.[17] To give another example, former Russian Railways head and still close Putin ally Vladimir Yakunin is active abroad. In Estonia, he contributed to the construction of an Orthodox cathedral in Tallinn and Edgar Savisaar's Centre Party, a handily divisive force in Estonian politics.[18] The World Public Forum Yakunin co-founded organises regular gatherings of senior current and former European leaders in Rhodes featuring a strongly anti-American agenda and set up its own think-tank in Berlin, the Dialogue of Civilisations.[19]

This also has an impact on Russia's relatively under-developed think-tank sector. While there are conspicuous exceptions such as the Carnegie Moscow Centre and the defence-oriented CAST, the majority is heavily dependent on either a relative handful of benefactors or, more usually, the state. Think-tanks, research centres and even public intellectuals such as the notorious Eurasianist-nationalist Alexander Dugin and fellow national-imperialist Alexander Prokhanov not only compete for government funds and favour, but also they may be used, whether for messaging or for more direct purposes as advocates, propagandists and deniable emissaries. For example, the Russian Institute of Strategic Studies (RISI) has become infamous in the Balkans not only for lobbying in Moscow for a more assertive Russian policy but also as a source of funds for certain local groups and a front for agents and agitators.[20] Part of the SVR until 2009, since then RISI has remained inexplicably well-resourced (it has a central office in Moscow and eight regional offices) and clearly close to the Presidential Administration and, it is widely assumed, to the SVR still.

God squad

The Moscow Patriarchate of the Russian Orthodox Church is inces-tuously connected with the Russian state. Traditionally, it upheld an alliance with the tsars, regarded as God's chosen rulers. In Soviet time, the Church was heavily penetrated by the KGB, and now it benefits from generous financial privileges. The current hierarchy under Patriarch Kirill – who began his career under the Soviets and has described Putin's presidency as a 'miracle of God' – appears delighted to con-tinue the relationship.[21] This extends beyond simply backing the regime at home to sanctifying and supporting its geopolitical programme, whether publicly blessing troops in Crimea or working alongside the foreign ministry to extend and assert Russian soft power. In Ukraine, for example, the Patriarchate is involved in a vicious political-religious struggle with the Kyiv Patriarchate, which in October 2018 received the permission of the Orthodox Ecumenical Patriarch in Turkey to become fully independent. Meanwhile in the Balkans, the Moscow Patriarchate is actively involved in reviving and strengthening historical and religious connections with local churches and congregations. Even its outreach to the Papacy has an inevitable political dimension, successfully keeping the Vatical talking about a 'civil war' in Ukraine rather than a Russian-instigated pseudo-rebellion.[22]

However, it is also important to remember that Russia is a multi-ethnic and multi-confessional nation, and while to some audiences the Kremlin emphasises its Christian foundations, elsewhere it is happy to spotlight its substantial Muslim population: Islam is the country's second most widely professed faith. Islamic institutions such as the Central Muslim Spiritual Board of Russia are used by the state to reinforce Putin's claims that Russia is and will remain a 'reliable ally' of the Muslim world.[23] In addition, Chechnya's unruly warlord, Ramzan Kadyrov, has also begun to emerge as an ambassador of sorts with the Islamic world.[24] Again, one should not presume this is solely or even mainly part of a Kremlin scheme, as Kadyrov is at best only partly under control. However, he is an increasingly active presence in the Islamic world, from his frequent visits to the royal families of Saudi Arabia, Bahrain and the United Arab Emirates to holding rallies in support of Muslim minorities in Myanmar.

NGOs and soft-power instruments

Moscow is painfully deficient in soft power – the capacity to influence through affection and positive example. To Western eyes, soft power does not fit into the context of active measures, but in Russian thinking, it is simply one more lever to influence other countries to one's own advantage. To the Russians, moreover, it is driven by state action, not civil society.[25] Often, Russian soft power is confined to national leaders to whom Putin's image as the model of the decisive modern autocrat appeals.[26] In south-east Europe, it can draw on shared religious faith in Bulgaria, Serbia and the like, but also an historical role as defender, not least against the Ottoman Empire. Elsewhere, Russia has a certain cachet, even if often for mythologised and misunderstood reasons, as an obstacle to supposed American hegemony or as a bastion of traditional values.

Organisations including *Rossotrudnichestvo* – the Federal Agency for the Commonwealth of Independent States, Compatriots Living

Abroad and International Humanitarian Cooperation – as well as notionally independent charities and other structures work specifically with Russian émigré communities.[27] *Rossotrudnichestvo* is subordinated to the foreign ministry, and from championing supposedly oppressed Russian minorities abroad to thundering against the iniquities of Western policy, it continues to be a powerful presence. For example, in 2016 the foreign ministry and its agencies paid for representatives of the Legal Information Centre for Human Rights and the Russian School in Estonia, two Kremlin-friendly NGOs, to take part in an annual OSCE meeting. Kapo, Estonia's Security Police, claims they 'painted a picture of Estonia that completely met the expectation of the sponsor – Estonia violates the rights of Russian children to be educated in their mother tongue and has a "massive" issue with people without citizenship, and so on.'[28] This was an operation jointly coordinated by the Russian embassy in Tallinn, and the ministry's Department for Relations with Compatriots Abroad, in Moscow.[29]

Whether oligarchs encouraged to bankroll soft-power projects, media outlets generating what the Russians call the *infoshum* ('infonoise') to drown out truth and certainty, or state-controlled or -influenced NGOs charged with advancing a partisan agenda, Putin's mobilisation state seeks to assemble all the resources it can, fully aware of the scale of the challenge it faces.

Notes

1 Conversation in Moscow, April 2017.
2 This chapter draws heavily on Mark Galeotti, *Controlling Chaos: How Russia Manages Its Political War in Europe* (ECFR, 2017), used with permission.
3 'Expanded meeting of the Government,' *Kremlin*, 31 January 2013 http://en.kremlin.ru/events/president/news/17396.
4 *Kommersant*, 7 April 2012.
5 For an only partial list of the most useful examples, see Ulrik Franke, *War by Non-military Means* (FOI, 2015); Peter Pomerantsev and Michael Weiss, *The Menace of Unreality: How the Kremlin Weaponizes Information, Culture and Money* (Institute of Modern Russia, 2014); James Sherr, *Hard Diplomacy and Soft Coercion: Russia's Influence Abroad* (Royal Institute of International Affairs, 2013).
6 BuzzFeed, 5 December 2013.
7 *New York Times*, 2 June 2015; 'One professional Russian troll tells all,' RFE/RL, 25 March 2015; *Guardian*, 2 April 2016.
8 Fredrik Wesslau, 'Putin's friends in Europe,' *ECFR Commentary*, 19 October 2016.

9 See, for example, RT, 1 March 2014.

10 BBC, 10 October 2016.

11 Christopher Paul and Miriam Matthews, 'The Russian "Firehose of Falsehood" propaganda model,' *RAND Perspective*, 2016 www.rand.org/pubs/perspectives/PE198.html.

12 For more on this, see Mark Galeotti and Anna Arutunyan, 'Hybrid business – the risks in the Kremlin's weaponization of the economy,' RFE/RL, 20 July 2016.

13 EurActiv, 4 December 2014.

14 Czech Radio, 23 January 2013. For a thoughtful assessment of Zeman's potential value to Moscow, see Sławomir Budziak, 'Czech echoes of the Kremlin's information war,' *New Eastern Europe*, 30 March 2015.

15 See Council Implementing Regulation (EU) No. 826/2014 https://eur-lex.europa.eu/legal-content/EN/TXT/?qid=1545080196107&uri=CELEX:320 14R0826; US Treasury, 'Treasury targets additional Ukrainian separatists and Russian individuals and entities,' 19 December 2014 www.treasury.gov/press-center/press-releases/Pages/jl9729.aspx.

16 *Zavtra*, 20 November 2014.

17 *Slon*, 19 May 2014; *Vedomosti*, 16 May 2014.

18 *Baltic Times*, 1 May 2011; Bloomberg, 2 March 2015.

19 *Financial Times*, 5 October 2016; *Deutsche Welle*, 1 July 2016.

20 For rival assessments of its importance, see Reuters, 19 April 2017, and *Moscow Times*, 20 April 2017.

21 Reuters, 8 February 2012.

22 *National Catholic Reporter*, 8 March 2016.

23 *Sovet Muftiev Rossii*, 26 May 2017 www.muslim.ru/en/articles/138/18364/; *Novosti*, 27 May 2016.

24 *Deutsche Welle*, 6 September 2016; *Wall Street Journal*, 21 September 2017.

25 Joseph Nye, 'What China and Russia don't get about soft power,' *Foreign Policy*, 29 April 2013.

26 *Financial Times*, 16 May 2016; 'Trump, Putin, Xi, and the return of kingship,' *The Diplomat*, 19 January 2017.

27 See Orysia Lutsevych, *Agents of the Russian World: Proxy Groups in the Contested Neighbourhood* (Chatham House, 2016).

28 *Estonian Internal Security Service Annual Review 2017* (Estonian Internal Security Service, 2017), p. 7 www.kapo.ee/en/content/annual-reviews.html.

29 Conversation with Russian foreign ministry staffer, March 2016.

Part IV
Facing the challenge

11 Welcome to the new world of war

Of course, there's nothing new in hybrid war. It's as old as the Trojan Horse. What distinguishes it is the fact that its scale is bigger, its speed and intensity are higher, and it's taking place on our borders.

(NATO Secretary-General Jens Stoltenberg, 2015)[1]

Like it or (probably) not, the West is at war, but not necessarily the kind of war it imagines or with which it is accustomed. It is already at war with Russia for the simple reason that it takes only one side to make a war, and the Kremlin has already made the decision that the West has started it. The Russians' reasoning is deeply questionable; we may debate how far Western naivety, cynicism, self-deception or hypocrisy are to blame; there is scope to consider what could and will be the way to end this civilisational and geopolitical clash. There is even ample room for scholars, semanticists and philosophers to decide if we even can call it 'war' when it is almost certainly not going to involve open armed conflict, rather than a shadowy tussle of politics, values, propaganda and mobilised and manipulated self-interest.

The overarching conclusions of this book are that while there is indeed something specific and dangerous about Russia's current nonlinear approach to war, the instruments they use are, in essence, neither. Deception and propaganda, coercive diplomacy and economic leverage, subversion and deniable auxiliaries have been tools of statecraft so long as there have been states. What is new is the world in which they are being employed, and it may well prove that where Russia leads, we all follow. Regardless of what happens in Moscow, whether or not Russia continues to be a strategic challenge (and it will, at least as long as Putin remains in power), this is an issue that needs serious attention.

Covert and ambiguous forces and agencies such as those described above should therefore be considered simply one of many potential weapons in the arsenal; as one Russian General Staff Academy instructor put it in a conversation, 'when the enemy already has a regiment in the field, you use artillery; when you want to strike before the enemy can deploy that regiment, or without his knowing he needs to, you use *gibridchiki*' – 'hybridists,' an ugly term, I am glad to say, I have not come across before or since.[2] However, when exploring Russian discussion of such 'sub-military' options, as well as their use, what emerges is an understanding is that there are sharply limited circumstances in which such instruments and approaches are truly useful.

Their main value is to lever open fault lines already present and exploit those failures of governance and security left by blunder, inaction or incapacity.[3] In Crimea, the annexation was not simply a matter of bluff and surprise, so much as taking advantage of an almost uniquely advantageous situation. The presence of Black Sea Fleet bases on the peninsula meant that Russian forces were already in place. Decades of neglect had left a Russophone population already disposed to a change in status, with a large organised-crime community closely linked to Russia. Kyiv was in disarray, its chain of command compromised and mistrusted. Although the long-term strategic success of the Donbas operation is still debatable, in the immediate term the Russians again exploited weaknesses in local control and governance. Besides, if in Crimea the aim was to create a new order, in the Donbas it was as much as anything else to create chaos, albeit a controlled, weaponised chaos.[4] However, the lessons of the Donbas are also that relying on active measures and deniable auxiliaries work well enough in the initial stages against an enemy still adapting and, in this case, recovering from virtual state collapse. However, they quickly become much less effective, and it is Russian artillery and armour, albeit largely based over the border, that represents the real force keeping the Donbas contested, not mercenaries and militias.

Taking the hype out of hybrid

So is talk of a 'new way of war' simply alarmist hyperbole? Damien Van Puyvelde certainly suggests so:

> So my recommendation is that NATO, and other Western decision-makers, should forget about everything 'hybrid' and focus on the specificity and the interconnectedness of the threats they face. Warfare, whether it be ancient or modern, hybrid or not, is always complex and can hardly be subsumed into a single adjective.[5]

This is a useful corrective, and it is certainly true that pretty much every conflict has been hybrid to some degree. However, there is something that is distinctive about the modern situation, even if not so much in essence, but in degree. This applies to both the essentially bloodless, if no less ruthless, political war, and the political-military hybrid war seen in Ukraine.

To a considerable extent, this is less about Russia, more about how nation-to-nation contestation is changing in a modern, interconnected, post-ideological world. First of all, conventional war has become extremely expensive and destructive. A Second World War P-51 Mustang fighter cost around $51,000 in 1945, equivalent to around $675,000 today; the current F-22 in service with the US Airforce costs around $340 million apiece.[6] Of course, the capabilities of the latter are similarly orders of magnitude higher, but the simple fact is that modern, high-tech war is prohibitively costly. It also has a far greater and perhaps even more important political price tag attached. Democratic electorates – and thus politicians seeking election – have shown themselves ever less willing to accept casualties lightly. The way the deaths of 241 US Marines in the 1983 Beirut barracks bombing, and later the 1993 'Black Hawk Down' incident in Mogadishu, contributed markedly to the early end of missions in Lebanon and Somalia respectively were several times raised by Russian analysts in conversation as evidence of this trend, magnified by the impact of the modern media. Yet this is not a trait confined to democracies. The Putin regime may essentially be an authoritarianism, but it also seeks to cultivate genuine legitimacy at home. Bloody foreign adventures are not popular, and casualties raise bitter memories of the terrible Chechen wars. The Kremlin's denials that Russian troops are in the Donbas and the use of mercenaries in Syria to keep down the official death toll may be as much about deceiving its own population as the West.

Second, the legal and geopolitical constraints on warfare are increasingly presenting both obstacles and opportunities. On the one hand, there demonstrably are not just reputational but real costs to open aggression, visible in the present sanctions regime. On the other hand, the flipside of this is the aforementioned lawfare, the wilful (ab)use of these structures for political gain.[7] In some ways, this is a perversely good sign: lawfare only makes sense if international law and perceptions of its breaches actually matter. In the meantime, though, it opens up a new arena for contestation, and also demonstrates that even countries such as Russia and China, often presented as outright foes of the global order, actually rather seek to use it to their advantage (in a way that they believe the West has, from the first).

Hybrid war

All this means that there are more reasons to turn to the military notion of hybrid war, as a complement or prelude to conventional, high-intensity conflict: when war is so risky and expensive, better to try and win it as quickly and bloodlessly as possible. However, even if war is likely to get smaller and sneakier, it is important to recognise the limits of such a military revolution. Nicu Popescu has suggested that hybrid war is dangerous because 'it is easy and cheap to launch for external aggressors, but costly in various ways for the defenders.'[8] This is, however, questionable. The historical lesson is actually that such tactics are unlikely to succeed unless the target has, to a considerable extent, already lost – at least in terms of losing its capacity or will to resist. In Estonia in 1924, for example, local Communists stiffened and organised by Soviet intelligence officers launched a coup, which was then intended to be the basis for an 'invitation' for fraternal 'assistance.' Soviet naval forces were already at sea, and ground forces mobilised on the pretext of a training exercise near the border. They initially managed to seize several key locations, but then the government galvanised itself and declared a state of emergency, the anticipated working-class support failed to materialise and the security forces began to reassert control.[9] While there is no question but that the Red Army could have conquered Estonia in a full invasion, rather than engage in an openly imperial venture, Moscow backed down. It pulled its covert operators from Estonia when it could, and disavowed any role in the attempted coup.

So, hybrid tactics offer no magic-bullet solution. When looking at a range of operations in other theatres in which an aggressor has tried to use covert or deniable military force, Dan Altman has noted that they usually fail, and they fail because of conventional force:

> In each instance, the defender countered hybrid tactics in the same way. They accepted the fictitious terms of the conflict and mobilized enough strength to defeat the deniable forces on the battlefield. They sought to engage the deniable forces without also attacking any uniformed forces of the aggressor or striking targets in the aggressor's territory, keeping the fighting contained. On the battlefield (although not in their rhetoric), both sides maintained the fiction that the conflict was something less than an open attack by the aggressor.[10]

Considering the perceptions and adventurist bent of Putin's regime, it is essential that the West still maintains forces able to deter and counter such operations, not so much because there is any evidence Moscow seriously seeks such a confrontation, but to ensure no such temptations may arise. While this necessarily involves something of a force realignment, reversing the West's pivot towards light, mobile out-of-area intervention forces, it is important to remember that it has massive underlying strengths in resources, technology and unity. We should not fall into the trap of over-stating Russian capacities. Moscow's *maskirovka* frequently seeks to intimidate and over-awe through projecting an exaggerated sense of its strength, hoping to demoralise and thus encourage concessions. So far Russia's actual military adventures have, we must remember, largely been under ideal or favourable circumstances and against far-from-peer adversaries.

In 2008, for example, the Russians – supported by thousands of Abkhazian and South Ossetian militias – faced the army of Georgia, just 35,000 strong, with some of its best troops serving at the time alongside the Coalition in Afghanistan. Even so, the Georgians were often able to outfight the Russians on a one-for-one basis.[11] Crimea was Moscow's for the picking, especially given the disinclination on Kyiv's part – sadly, encouraged by Washington[12] – not to order its troops to resist. There, as in the Donbas, the Russians only sent professionals, and often from elite units, at that. As is, the constant search for professionals is behind the use of scratch-built, compound battalion tactical groups in the war, with inevitable challenges to unit cohesion. In Syria, the Russians are still largely fighting an air war against an enemy with minimal anti-air capacity. In short, these wars of choice have also been fought with a stacked deck, and there is no reason to believe Moscow is willing to play on other terms if it has a choice.

The West's real threat: political war

Hybrid and political war depend on exploiting vulnerabilities, especially ones relating to unity, will and the capacity to resist. As András Rácz observes:

> Hybrid warfare is built on capitalizing on the weaknesses of a country, on flaws in its political system, administration, economy and society. If an adversary cannot detect sufficient weaknesses, then no full-scale attack can be launched, meaning that hybrid warfare never reaches the second, attack phase. Hence, the best defence against hybrid warfare is good governance.[13]

These instruments are thus most applicable to countries experiencing political and social turmoil, with low or diminishing legitimacy of the existing order, and also weak security structures. Most European countries may suffer from one or two of these from time to time, but rarely all three at once. The more plausible targets for true hybrid war are within Russia's 'Near Abroad.' Georgia has already been the target of kinetic-political operations and may still be facing information- and economic-vectored aggression. Moldova remains vulnerable, and Kazakhstan may prove so in the future given the presence of ethnic Russians in the north, if the long-awaited Nazarbaev succession dismays Moscow and creates domestic disarray.

Besides which, hybrid war by definition is intended to lead to full, conventional conflict, and while it is possible to dream up scenarios whereby NATO's Article 5 guarantee is not or cannot be activated, there seems no hunger in Moscow to risk war with the West, and no political, let alone territorial, objectives worthy of the massive risks involved. At its 2014 Wales Summit, NATO grappled with the new challenge and produced some welcome initiatives such as the approval of the Readiness Action Plan.

However, the real question is, in many ways, how far this is a truly military issue. NATO is well placed to respond to direct kinetic threats, and Putin was probably speaking for his entire security elite when he said: 'I think that only someone who has lost their mind or is in a dream could imagine that Russia would one day attack NATO.'[14] It is worth noting that in my contact with Russian officers and security staffers, time and again it became clear that however worried Westerners may be about the value of NATO's Article 5 mutual-defence guarantee, the Russians appear to take it very seriously indeed. For this very reason, it is unlikely that Moscow would even pose any such challenge, at least not unless the political context changes dramatically. Instead, Russia could use intelligence, political and economic tactics beyond NATO's remit. In short, the real threat to the West is not hybrid but political war, which is, after all, the other logical response to the changing costs of war as well as the new instabilities of the modern age: achieve your objectives by aggressive and sometimes violent political operations that still stay below the true threshold of outright military action.

Notes

1 Speech at the opening of the NATO Transformation Seminar, 25 March 2015 www.nato.int/cps/en/natohq/opinions_118435.htm.
2 Conversation, Moscow, January 2016.

3 For an interesting exploration of Russians' successes and limitations, see James Sherr, *Hard Diplomacy and Soft Coercion: Russia's Influence Abroad* (Royal Institute of International Affairs, 2013).

4 Mark Galeotti, ' "Hybrid war" and "little green men": how it works, and how it doesn't,' in Agnieszka Pikulicka-Wilczewska and Richard Sakwa (eds), *Ukraine and Russia: People, Politics, Propaganda and Perspectives* (e-IR Press, 2015), pp. 156–164.

5 Damien Van Puyvelde, 'Hybrid war – does it even exist?' *NATO Review*, 2015.

6 *The National Interest*, 30 August 2016.

7 This is a growing field of study in both scholarly and policy circles; see Charles Dunlap, 'Lawfare: a decisive element of 21st-century conflicts?' *Joint Force Quarterly*, 54 (2009); Orde Kittrie, *Lawfare: Law as a Weapon of War* (Oxford University Press, 2016).

8 Nicu Popescu, 'Hybrid tactics: neither new nor only Russian,' *European Union Institute for Security Studies*, January 2015.

9 Merle Maigre, 'Nothing new in hybrid warfare: the Estonian experience and recommendations for NATO,' *German Marshall Fund of the United States Policy Brief*, February 2015.

10 Dan Altman, 'The long history of "green men" tactics – and how they were defeated,' War on the Rocks, 17 March 2016 https://warontherocks.com/2016/03/the-long-history-of-green-men-tactics-and-how-they-were-defeated/.

11 Ariel Cohen and Robert Hamilton, *The Russian Military and the Georgia War: Lessons and Implications* (Strategic Studies Institute, 2011); Michael Kofman, 'Russian performance in the Russo-Georgian war revisited,' War on the Rocks, 4 September 2018 https://warontherocks.com/2018/09/russian-performance-in-the-russo-georgian-war-revisited/.

12 Bloomberg, 21 August 2015.

13 András Rácz, *Russia's Hybrid War in Ukraine* (Finnish Institute of International Affairs, 2015), p. 92.

14 *Corriere della Sera*, 6 June 2015.

12 Fighting (defensive) political war

> What the Russians understood in Crimea is that it's easy to take over territory when its people don't want to stay. We should have fought for Crimea, but we should have fought for its peoples' loyalty in the twenty years before, too. Then, they might have fought for us.
>
> (Ukrainian security official, 2015)[1]

In a telling echo of that Ukrainian's rueful admission, a just-retired Russian officer in the General Staff's Main Operations Directorate told me that 'had [Kyiv] fought in Crimea, they might not now be fighting in the Donbas.'[2] One could suggest that actually, instead of destabilisation being primarily an annex of military action, it was rather that only because of political weakness did more aggressive moves become thinkable, even – from the Kremlin's perspective – necessary.

The modern West – networked, globally integrated, concerned with multiple real and perceived threats, and facing underlying crises of confidence and legitimacy – has specific vulnerabilities that the Russians are eagerly exploiting. The fundamental challenges are to understand quite what this involves, what Russia's capabilities are, and what can be done to deter and respond to it. This is no quick or easy matter, especially as the threat facing the West is political, not hybrid war, unless one side or the other makes some particularly bad decisions. The challenge of responding to the non-kinetic challenge is even more intractable. Should information warfare based on propaganda and spin be counteracted with more propaganda, with fact-checkers or through media awareness classes in schools?[3] For countries with potentially fractious minorities that Moscow could exploit, is the most effective way of buying security to spend more on counter-intelligence officers, police and social inclusion programmes, rather than to buy tanks or aircraft?

Addressing this challenge can no more be the sole preserve of the soldier as it is of the diplomat or the counter-intelligence officer. Instead, what will be needed is a coordinated, all-of-government response that addresses legitimacy gaps and media awareness as assiduously as military capabilities and spycatching. As former NATO supreme commander General Philip Breedlove put it, 'in Ukraine, what we see is ... diplomatic tools being used, informational tools being used, military tools being used, economic tools being used against Ukraine ... We, I think, in the West, should consider all of our tools in reply.'[4]

Deterrence by denial

> [T]he way I describe the role of the military ... is to make us immune from coercion, make the nation immune from coercion.
>
> (General Martin Dempsey, former Chairman of the US Joint Chiefs of Staff, 2014)[5]

Drawing on Russian strategic thinking, though, what implications does this have for present security calculi?[6] If anything, the West should again turn to Gerasimov, this time a 2014 speech to the Russian Academy of Military Sciences. He called for a 'comprehensive set of strategic defence measures embracing the entire state apparatus ... to convince potential aggressors of the futility of any forms of pressure on the Russian Federation and its allies.'[7] The West ought to take a leaf from Moscow's book, and see how, without sacrificing its democratic values and liberties, it too can mobilise to deter or defeat any *gibridnye* threats.

As Rácz says, the main defence against such forms of warfare is thus pre-emptive, to 'target harden' by shoring up governance and legitimacy – a hybrid and political defence to resist hybrid and political war – sufficient to deny Moscow the hope of an easy victory.[8] This is the essence of deterrence by denial: relying not on a counter-threat so much as measures that make any attack unlikely to succeed. Of course, spooks, *Spetsnaz* and sympathisers will remain useful instruments in peace, for gathering intelligence, inspiring video games and influencing policy, respectively. However, none of these can fully compensate for essential weaknesses in military and economic strength. They are powerful means of magnifying existing shortfalls in will and capacity and taking full advantages of any opportunities that may emerge as a result, but they are still asymmetric assets, weapons of the weak.[9]

The good news is that the measures that can reduce the threat of a subversion-then-soldiers hybrid war are also effective against political war. This means adopting a more systematic approach to minimising vulnerabilities: 'fixing the roof' rather than simply hoping the rain will stop or seeking to bat away the storm, drop by drop. Without falling into the trap of securitising everything – which both securitises nothing and would also undermine the very values the West seeks to protect[10] – issues such as corruption, the presence of Russian-based organised crime, media regulation and bank secrecy all need to be considered in the context of national defence.

That means police and security services with adequate powers, budgets and skills to identify and, in turn, convict or expel agents, provocateurs, political operators and those who would fund and stir up divisive local movements. There is a huge variation in countries' spending on counter-intelligence, as well as their willingness to act on their security services' findings. Countries such as the UK and Estonia are spending several times more as a proportion of GDP on intelligence than, for example, Hungary, Portugal or Norway.[11] This affects not just national but continental security, as Russian agents use the freedoms of the Schengen zone to operate beyond their base country. Officials believe that Russian agents based in Hungary and the Czech Republic, just to take two examples, roam deep into Germany, Poland and beyond.[12] Just as NATO is the primary driver for pressing European countries to reach the alliance's 2% of GDP defence spending target, so too the West could look to create minimum measures of intelligence and counter-intelligence spending.

Above all, it means social outreach and a strong emphasis on governance and legitimacy. After all, corruption, the exclusion of minorities and communities – not just Russian-speakers – and public disillusion all create crucial opportunities for Moscow to exploit. The countries at most risk are largely characterised by weak (and sometimes weakening) institutions and low levels of trust in their own and transnational governance. Russia eagerly exploits these vulnerabilities, but cannot create them, so dealing with them ought to be considered a security priority, not just a political issue.[13] The democratic backsliding visible in Hungary and Poland, for example, not only risks opening up these countries to Russian influence operations but also generates Europe-wide vulnerabilities. Likewise, the discontents of specific regions and communities, dissatisfaction with national elites and similar issues undermining national and EU legitimacy need to be considered in this light. Obviously, this does not make blocking or undermining Russian propaganda campaigns designed to spread division and uncertainty any less important, or protecting the freedoms and transparency of domestic and international media. As James Sherr affirms: 'A free media should not be defenceless in the face of trolling, state-sponsored manipulation and cyber attack.'[14]

Maintaining social cohesion in the face of Russian covert assaults is not just a passive measure. In countries such as Lithuania, civil disobedience and other non-violent protests are being mooted as weapons against hybrid aggression.[15] It is even more important to consider positive strategies to mobilise civil society in the name of genuine national unity. This does not mean witch-hunts against supposed Russian agents and dupes, a dangerously divisive and McCarthyite tendency already visible in some quarters. This only fosters paranoias, shattering rather than cohering communities in a way that only plays to the Kremlin's own propaganda. The aim must be to fight gullibility, not disinformation, and this often means allowing marginal voices to be heard. Suppressing debate is the mark of authoritarianisms and does nothing genuinely to close national divisions. Instead, although a long-term approach, it is important to educate national populations to be more critical of media of every kind (by no means just that ostensibly relating to Russia) and easy answers to difficult modern challenges. No amount of 'myth-busting' of specific lies and counter-propaganda, let alone the silencing of inconvenient voices, can be as effective in addressing this fundamental challenge of the information age.[16]

Finally, it means proper controls on the flows of money from Russia, even if laundered through thinly veiled front companies in third-party jurisdictions. This money otherwise can be used to buy influence, support local political movements intended to stir up trouble, and take over strategic business sectors. Arguably, it is corruption rather than disinformation that is the most important political weapon that can be used against the West, targeting as it does the dominant rather than the disenfranchised, and undermining the legitimacy of their states. It is hardly coincidental that the populists now ascendant in the West have in so many ways based their appeal on the corruption of the status quo in one form or another, whether unelected 'Eurocrats' in Brussels or the 'swamp' inside the Washington, DC 'beltway.' This is, of course, a political issue, but it is often rooted in assumptions about the economic corruption of those in power, assumptions that are depressingly often not unfounded. No country likes turning away business, but in the modern world, money is weaponised, and Moscow understands this well.[17]

Governance is the new battlefield

None of these are new suggestions and all are being discussed, even if not always addressed with necessary will and resources. However, they are rarely considered as part of a comprehensive national security strategy. Nor do they fall within NATO's traditional remit. That is understandable, as is the generals' preference to stick to familiar measures such as the creation of the new Very High Readiness Joint Task Force. That is a necessary component of both the military and political defence of the West, but, beyond that, it cannot be NATO's job to audit banking probity in Latvia, say, or push social inclusion in Romania.

A recent Pew Research Centre poll found 27% of Europeans expressed doubts about NATO, even though 57% were in favour.[18] That over a quarter were uncomfortable cannot simply be hand-waved away as the result of ignorance or Russian disinformation. Addressing these doubts and winning back the doubtful is as important a security challenge as increasing defence budgets, and arguably an even more complex one. In part, this is a challenge for NATO as an institution, but the primary role will have to be played by national governments, including those that to date have been reluctant to champion the alliance to lukewarm electorates.

However, it also creates an opportunity for the EU, which has long been more interested in governance than war.[19] The most powerful defences against Russian mischief-making and manipulation are social cohesion, effective law enforcement, an independent and responsible media, honest and properly regulated financial institutions, and legitimate, transparent and effective governance. Beyond the existing Joint Framework adopted in April 2016,[20] a more strategic and urgent approach to ensuring these are found throughout the EU is thus a security necessity and not just a public good. Along with its External Action Service, responsible for common foreign policy, there is greater scope for structures not trying to parallel or challenge NATO on the kinetic side of defence, but rather to coordinate non-military defences, incorporating bodies such as Europol and the new East StratCom counter-propaganda group.

Member states need to be imaginative and flexible when they consider the challenges they face and how best they can be resisted. A simple increase in the defence budget may not always in itself be the most appropriate response. A country may need forensic accountants, media analysts or language teachers more than new missiles. At the risk of making the generals unhappy, as noted above, this may even mean that NATO should revisit its goal of having all members spend 2% of GDP on (conventional) defence, so long as they demonstrably are spending the shortfall on other security objectives. It is, after all, through such hybrid defence that the long-term challenge from the Kremlin will best be neutralised.

Political counter-attack?

Faced with Russia's undoubted political aggression, it is inevitable that – as in the Cold War – there are voices in the West calling for retaliation in kind. In July 2018, for example, the US Congress saw a provision added to the dissenting conference report on the John S. McCain National Defense Authorization Act for Fiscal Year 2019, which said the drafters had been 'disappointed with the past responses of the executive branch to adversary cyberattacks' and wanted the government to 'conduct aggressive information operations to deter adversaries.'[21]

It certainly makes sense to hone weapons of political war and also to demonstrate them, for deterrent value. These range from economic sanctions to means of countering Russian propaganda at home and abroad, including such existing services as the US RFE/RL and British BBC. However, they also include more covert and aggressive options, such as cyberattacks and political subversion. Edward Lucas, for example, has proposed running financial snap exercises:

> [W]ar games, but without kinetic weapons. We would assemble teams of decision-makers to rehearse the freezing and seizing of Russian assets at very short notice, in response to some (hypothetical but plausible) dangerous or provocative step by the Kremlin. This would involve combining intelligence inputs, the criminal justice system, financial regulators and our forensic capabilities quickly and precisely—and doing so in many countries, inside and outside the European Union and NATO. That in itself would be a useful exercise in teamwork. Even more useful would be spotting the obstacles, in order to iron them out in time for the next exercise.[22]

A key point is to demonstrate not just international solidarity but the capacity to field political 'combined arms.' None of Russia's gambits operate in isolation: threatening rhetoric, military deployments, covert subversion and media spin work most effectively precisely when they work together. By the same token, Western responses ought not to focus on a single medium – whether scrambling fighters or issuing statements – but work on a similar multi-platform basis. A demonstrative military response, for example, ought to be combined with a confident and pro-active media and political campaign explaining its need to domestic constituencies and emphasising its scale to the Kremlin. It should also highlight the West's other, specific advantages. Just as Moscow has already begun integrating domestic security agencies and even the Central Bank into its wargames,[23] so too exercises geared to exploring and demonstrating how putative Russian hostilities would be met should also, as Lucas suggests, explicitly incorporate offensive economic, cyber and even subversion and sabotage operations, compared with the present practice that largely confines itself to practising responding to such challenges. Of course, no one need be so impolite as to call the enemies 'Russians.' But just as Moscow holds its aggressive exercises behind a tissue-thin screen of deniability, relying on Europe to draw the right lessons, so too the West can play the same game. If Moscow screams 'provocation,' then it is actually evidence of success.

Most responses to Russian active measures have been limited and unimaginative, typically restricted to personal sanctions against those identified as directly involved, whether expelling spies, revoking press credentials or broad economic sanctions that hit ordinary Russians at least as much as Putin. In Moscow, the lack of clear and strong responses has been considered a sign of weakness and an inducement to continue: 'we really have no reason not to carry on as we are,' mused one recently retired General Staff officer, albeit in 2017, before the unexpectedly severe and cooperative expulsions of Russian diplomats following the Skripal case.[24] Without being needlessly provocative, Western countries should develop a strategy for consistent and meaningful retaliations. A key point is that they need not be mechanically symmetrical, defined by the form of interference. A disinformation campaign can be punished through targeted sanctions of political leaders, or illegal payments to extremist groups by providing extra aid to third parties facing Russian aggression. This is, after all, a campaign driven by the Russian state, and thus any arm of the state is fair game for retaliation. The aim is to identify pain points and apply pressure.

Furthermore, much more can be done through the use of sanctions to expose, punish and isolate specific individuals, the officials and 'adhocrats' acting as initiators, cheerleaders and 'curators' for Russian adventures. Following the Crimean annexation, this was the first approach adopted. From personal experience of living in Moscow at the time, the chilling effect this had on the elite was clear. When the emphasis shifted to sectoral economic sanctions, the sense of relief was palpable. The practice of personal sanctions, including freezing property and – despite some legal challenges – also targeting individuals' families, is one that not only gives a clear signal to the elite of the cost of being involved in Putin's political war, but it is also a message to the Russian people that Europe is not opposed to them, but to the corrupt Russian government. This does not necessarily mean targeting rich Russians as such – the notion that hitting the oligarchs punishes Putin is a crucial misreading of the situation, as it actually drives them back into his arms – but those, often officials, who have demonstrably particular roles within the active measures campaigns.

Blowback

However, to go further, to succumb to the temptation of waging a political war against Russia, would be a dangerous move. Of course, Russia has many vulnerabilities that could be exploited, from its dependence on imported food (that makes up almost a quarter of the total[25]) to the poor security of much of its physical and electronic infrastructure.

Moscow rationalises its political war by claiming that the West started it. In a telling irony, it may be that its very 'counter-attack' will actually spark such a Western campaign, albeit political rather than hybrid. This may legitimise Putin's narrative, but it is also likely to demonstrate just how vulnerable an over-geared, under-invested, over-securitised and under-legitimate Russia may be to the very tactics it uses so profligately. From cyberattacks to deeper and broader sanctions, launching propaganda campaigns to encouraging elite conspiracies, should they want to, the United States and its allies have formidable opportunities to fight their own political war inside Russia. Alarmist rhetoric aside, the 'new way of war' may well prove to be more of a threat to Russia than to the West.

But there is always a danger when policy is driven by opportunity not outcomes. The West has demonstrated that it is much better at effecting regime change than controlling the outcomes when it comes to its military adventures in Afghanistan, Iraq and Libya. This would likely be true of any aggressive political war against the Kremlin. However tempting some may find the thought of deposing Putin or otherwise taking the offensive, this could so easily backfire in a number of different ways. It could fail and turn a Russian leader whose popularity is already waning into a national icon. It could force a Kremlin leadership that felt it had nothing to lose into some desperate, destructive military adventure. Or it could succeed, and lead to the rise of an angry, nationalistic Russia. At the moment, after all, one could suggest that part of the reason for the Kremlin's constant and strident domestic propaganda is precisely because ordinary Russians do not naturally see the West as a threat to the same extent as Putin and his cronies, or feel enthusiasm for aggressive policies abroad. My personal view is that Putin represents a transitional leader, a last gasp of *homo Sovieticus* and the generation grappling with the end of empire and great-power status. History is dragging Russia where it belongs, into Europe, and while true democracy will likely take political generations to take root, Western arrogance and interference would most probably do more harm than good. Political war is, as Putin may be discovering, a much better tactic than a strategy.

Because who is actually 'winning'? Putin may seem to be doing the running, but as of the time of writing, while the West is grappling with Brexit, populism and transatlantic tensions, it is also essentially rich, secure and stable. Moscow is bogged down in the Donbas and likely Syria, politically isolated, economically sanctioned and with few options to improve its lot. Furthermore, adventurist moves such as interference in the 2016 US elections, attempted assassination in the UK and widespread hacking are all leading to calls for a more robust Western response. Whatever the concerns about the Trump presidency, there can be no question but that the US and Western national security establishment is more and more aware of the potential threat from Russian non-linear warfare. Is the real lesson of the current situation that hybrid and political war actually doesn't work as intended? Or at the very least, that it is not this war-winning masterplan for the underdog, as feared and hyped? Russia is at least as greatly at risk from unconstrained political warfare as the West, and while weaponising chaos can be a very powerful instrument, it is not only a weapon of the weak. Mutually assured destruction, the basis for nuclear deterrence since the middle of the last century, may well end up offering lessons also for this age of political warfare.

Notes

1 Conversation, London, July 2015. When asked to clarify, he launched into a lengthy critique of Ukrainian government policy towards Crimea under successive administrations.
2 Conversation, Moscow, May 2015.
3 Peter Pomerantsev and Michael Weiss, *The Menace of Unreality: How the Kremlin Weaponizes Information, Culture and Money* (Institute of Modern Russia, 2014).
4 DOD News, 23 March 2015.
5 Interviewed in War on the Rocks, 25 February 2014 https://warontherocks.com/2014/02/a-conversation-with-the-chairman-general-martin-e-dempsey/.
6 This section draws heavily on my 'Time to think about "hybrid defense",' War on the Rocks, 30 July 2015 https://warontherocks.com/2015/07/time-to-think-about-hybrid-defense/.
7 Valerii Gerasimov, 'Generalnyi shtab i oborona strany,' *Voenno-promyshlennyi kur'er*, 5 February 2014.

8 See, for example, Aapo Cederberg and Pasi Eronen, 'How can societies be defended against hybrid threats?' *GCSP Security Sector Analysis*, September 2015.
9 A term popularised by James C. Scott in his *Weapons of the Weak: Everyday Forms of Resistance* (Yale University Press, 1985).
10 For a useful warning, see Benjamin Tallis and Michal Šimečka, 'Collective defence in the age of hybrid warfare,' *IIR Discussion Paper*, 2016 www.dokumenty-iir.cz/DiscussionPapers/Discussion_paper_B_Tallis_2_TR.pdf.
11 For preliminary data, see Mark Galeotti, 'Trump was right: NATO is obsolete,' *Foreign Policy*, 20 July 2017.
12 Conversation with Czech BIS counter-intelligence officer in Prague, June 2017, and EU official, Brussels, June 2016; *index*, 21 March 2017; Lili Bayer, 'Moscow spooks return to Hungary, raising NATO hackles,' *Politico*, 19 July 2017.
13 'Hybrid war as a war on governance', *Small Wars Journal*, 19 August 2015 http://smallwarsjournal.com/jrnl/art/hybrid-war-as-a-war-on-governance.
14 James Sherr, *The New East–West Discord. Russian Objectives, Western Interests* (Clingendael, 2015), p. 74.
15 Maciej Bartkowski, 'Countering hybrid war: civil resistance as a national defence strategy,' *openDemocracy*, 12 May 2015.
16 Reid Standish, 'Why is Finland able to fend off Putin's information war?' *Foreign Policy*, 1 March 2017.
17 *Business Insider*, 5 January 2015.
18 Pew Research Centre, 'Support for NATO is widespread among member nations,' 6 July 2016.
19 See Peter Pindják, 'Deterring hybrid warfare: a chance for NATO and the EU to work together?,' *NATO Review*, 2015.
20 A programme directed towards raising awareness of the risks, building resilience by addressing potential strategic and critical sectors (including cybersecurity, critical infrastructures, protection of the financial system, protection of public health, and supporting efforts to counter violent extremism and radicalisation), crisis response, and increased cooperation within the EU and between the EU and NATO. It is, however, still a relatively vague commitment involving sharing papers and joint meetings more than anything more concrete. European Commission, 'Security: EU strengthens response to hybrid threats,' 6 April 2016 http://europa.eu/rapid/press-release_IP-16-1227_en.htm.
21 *John S. McCain National Defense Authorization Act for Fiscal Year 2019 – Conference Report to Accompany H.R. 5515*, July 2018, scts 1642 and 1633 https://docs.house.gov/billsthisweek/20180723/CRPT-115hrpt863.pdf.
22 Edward Lucas, 'Deterrence and "financial snap exercises",' *CEPA Europe's Edge*, 6 February 2018.
23 TASS, 9 September 2016.
24 Conversation, Moscow, April 2017.
25 Galina Mikhailovna Zinchuk et al., 'Food security of Russia in the context of import substitution,' *European Research Studies Journal*, 20, 3 (2017).

Select bibliography

Bērziņš, Jānis, 'Russian new generation warfare is not hybrid warfare,' in Artis Pabriks and Andis Kudors (eds), *The War in Ukraine: Lessons for Europe* (University of Latvia Press, 2015), pp. 40–51.

Bukkvoll, Tor, 'Military innovation under authoritarian government – the case of Russian special operations forces,' *Journal of Strategic Studies*, 38, 5 (2015), pp. 602–625.

Chekinov, Sergei and Sergei Bogdanov, 'Vliyanie nepriamykh deistvii na kharakter sovremennoi voiny,' *Voennaya mysl'*, June 2011.

Cohen, Ariel and Robert Hamilton, *The Russian Military and the Georgia War: Lessons and Implications* (Strategic Studies Institute, 2011).

Frank, Ulrike, *War by Non-military Means* (FOI, 2015).

Freedman, Lawrence, 'Ukraine and the art of limited war,' *Survival*, 56, 6 (2014), pp. 7–38.

Fridman, Ofer, *Russian 'Hybrid Warfare'* (Hurst, 2018).

Galeotti, Mark, 'Hybrid, ambiguous, and non-linear? How new is Russia's "new way of war"?' *Small Wars & Insurgencies*, 27, 2 (2016), pp. 282–301.

Galeotti, Mark, *Putin's Hydra: Inside Russia's Intelligence Services* (ECFR, 2016) www.ecfr.eu/publications/summary/putins_hydra_inside_russias_intelligence_services.

Galeotti, Mark, *Controlling Chaos: How Russia Manages Its Political War in Europe* (ECFR, 2017) www.ecfr.eu/publications/summary/controlling_chaos_how_russia_manages_its_political_war_in_europe.

Gareev, Makhmut, *Esli zavtra voina* (Vladar, 1995).

Gerasimov, Valerii, 'Tsennost' nauki v predvidenii.' *Voenno-promyshlennyi kur'er*, 27 February 2013.

Giles, Keir, *Russia's 'New' Tools for Confronting the West: Continuity and Innovation in Moscow's Exercise of Power* (Chatham House, 2016).

Hoffman, Frank, *Conflict in the Twenty-first Century: the Rise of Hybrid Warfare* (Potomac Institute, 2000).

Hoffman, Frank, 'On not-so-new warfare: political warfare vs hybrid threats,' War on the Rocks, 28 July 2014 http://warontherocks.com/2014/07/on-not-so-new-warfare-political-warfare-vs-hybrid-threats/.

Howard, Colby and Ruslan Pukhov (eds), *Brothers Armed: Military Aspects of the Crisis in Ukraine, 2nd edition* (EastView Press, 2015).

Isserson, Georgii, *Evolutsiya operativnogo iskusstva* (Voenizdat, 1937).

Jonsson, Oscar and Robert Seely, 'Russian full-spectrum conflict: an appraisal after Ukraine,' *Journal of Slavic Military Studies*, 28, 1 (2015), pp. 1–22.

Kofman, Michael, 'Russian hybrid warfare and other dark arts,' War on the Rocks, 11 March 2016 http://warontherocks.com/2016/03/russian-hybrid-warfare-and-other-dark-arts/.

Lasconjarias, Guillaume and Jeffrey Larsen (eds), *NATO's Response to Hybrid Threats* (NATO Defense College, 2015).

Liang, Qiao and Wang Xiangsui, *Unrestricted Warfare* (Pan-American Publishing Company, 2002).

Madeira, Victor, *Britannia and the Bear: The Anglo-Russian Intelligence Wars, 1917–1929* (Boydell, 2014).

Maigre, Merle, 'Nothing new in hybrid warfare: the Estonian experience and. recommendations for NATO,' *German Marshall Fund of the United States Policy Brief*, February 2015.

Monaghan, Andrew, *Russian State Mobilization: Moving the Country on to a War Footing* (Chatham House, 2016).

Nemeth, Douglas, 'Future war and Chechnya: a case for hybrid warfare,' Naval Postgraduate School, Monterey, CA, Master's thesis (2002) http://calhoun. nps.edu/bitstream/handle/10945/5865/02Jun_Nemeth.pdf?sequence=1.

Pomerantsev, Peter and Michael Weiss, *The Menace of Unreality: How the Kremlin Weaponizes Information, Culture and Money* (Institute of Modern Russia, 2014).

Pukhov, Ruslan, 'Mif o "gibridnoi voine",' *Nezavisimoe voennoe obozrenie*, 29 May 2015.

Rácz, András, *Russia's Hybrid War in Ukraine* (Finnish Institute of International Affairs, 2015).

Renz, Bettina, 'Russia and "hybrid warfare",' *Contemporary Politics*, 22, 3 (2016), pp. 283–300.

Savinkin, A. E. and I. V. Domnin (eds), *Groznoe oruzhie: Malaya voina, partizanstvo i drugie vidy asimmetrichnogo voevaniya v svete naslediya russkikh voennykh myslitelei* (Russkii put', 2007).

Seely, Robert, *A Definition of Contemporary Russian Conflict: How Does the Kremlin Wage War?* (Henry Jackson Society, 2018).

Sherr, James, *Hard Diplomacy and Soft Coercion: Russia's Influence Abroad* (Royal Institute of International Affairs, 2013).

Thomas, Timothy, 'Russia's military strategy and Ukraine: indirect, asymmetric – and Putin-led,' *Journal of Slavic Military Studies*, 28, 3 (2015), pp. 445–461.

Vladimirov, Alexander, *Kontseptualnye osnovy natsionalnoi strategii Rossii: Voyennopoliticheskii aspekt* (Nauka, 2007).

Index

For Product Safety Concerns and Information please contact our
EU representative GPSR@taylorandfrancis.com Taylor & Francis
Verlag GmbH, Kaufingerstraße 24, 80331 München, Germany